Speak Scotch
Or Whistle

Also by Albert Mackie:

TALKING GLASGOW

'It claims on the cover that the reader will "Laugh out loud" — I for one won't be suing for breach of promise.'

The Scots Magazine

'Anyone who doesn't raise at least a few smiles at this should have his funny bone retreaded.'

Dundee Evening Telegraph

'...dialect, thank Goad, is alive and well and living in Glasgow.'

Edinburgh Evening News

SPEAK SCOTCH OR WHISTLE

Albert Mackie

Illustrations by
John MacKay

BLACKSTAFF PRESS

12099

ISBN 0 85640 192 7

Printed in Great Britain by Billing and Sons Ltd, Guildford, London, Oxford and Worcester.

Contents

Even the Prince of Wales gets into the act

It was my grandfather Andrew Gibson whom I first heard use the phrase: 'Speak Scotch or whistle!'

He was a baker to trade, with a hooked nose, a close-cropped iron-grey moustache and a chin stubble which disappeared on a Saturday when he paid his weekly visit to the barber.

'Awndray', as his Christian name was pronounced in Lothian and the Borders, used to tell us he came from 'Burdiehoose' or 'Burdie'. It is on the map as Burdiehouse, a corruption of Bordeaux, for it was at one time a French colony south of Edinburgh, but is now a vastly built-up suburb of the Scottish capital.

In fact I believe he was born in the Borders, somewhere about Lauder, but had spent part of his youth in 'Burdie'. He spoke what he called 'Scotch' with a strong Border accent, and if any of the scholars of today, who prefer 'Scots' or 'Scottish', had said to him; 'Andrew, old chap, you don't *speak* Scotch, you *drink* it,' he would have replied without hesitation, 'Thank ye kindly, Ah dinnae mind if Ah div.'

If he was wrong in his use of the word, he erred in distinguished company, including Robert Burns, Sir Walter Scott, Lord Byron (a Gordon of Gight) and Sir James Wilson, a great authority on the language, who was active in my grandfather's day, and entitled his most famous book *Lowland Scotch*.

However, what my grandfather meant when he said 'Speak Scotch or whistle!' was simply: 'Use plain language, and dinnae gie'z ony o' yer lang-nebbit words!' It was when I was suffering from undigested higher education, and expressing myself in abstractions of Latin and Greek origin, that he would bring me to a jerky halt with his favourite phrase.

He was by no means anticipating Hugh MacDiarmid and the Scottish Renaissance, or suggesting that I should speak Scots rather than English. All he wanted was that I should use words both of us would understand.

Most of what I knew of the old language I had learned not so much

7

at his knee as *on* it. For when I was very young he had dandled me on his knee to the rhythm of his recitation:

'John Smith, felly fine,
Can ye shae a horse o' mine?
Yes, sir, and that Ah can,
Jist as weel as ony man.
Pit a bit upon the tae,
Tae gar the powny sclim the brae;
Pit a bit upon the midst
Tae gar the powny skip the dubs;
Pit a bit upon the heel
Tae gar the powny pace weel,
Pace weel, pace weel.'

'Shae' and 'felly' was how he pronounced 'shoe' and 'fellow', and the verse from the fifth line meant: 'Put a bit upon the toe, to make the pony climb the hill; put a bit upon the middle to make the pony skip over the puddles; put a bit upon the heel to make the pony pace well!'

As he reeled it off, he used to pound his clenched fist against the sole of my shoe to suggest the blacksmith driving in the nails. This performance had been a must on all his calls in from the bakehouse on his way home.

Another was his imitation of a train going through the Waverley tunnel, which he effected by taking a deep draw of his thick black pipe tobacco and letting the smoke issue slowly from his half-open mouth. By rubbing his chin against our infant cheeks, he gave us what he called 'bairdie'.

He had a wealth of old Scottish phrases and sayings which he had passed on to my mother, so that even when he was no longer with us his words still echoed in our home.

'Ach! Thae folk are feared for the day they never saw.'
'Ah'm no sae green as Ah'm cabbage-lookin.'
'He never said: "Collie, wid ye lick?"'
'A wink's as guid as a nod tae a blin horse.'
'A stoot hert tae a stey brae.'
'Giffgaff maks guid freens.'
'We never dee'd a winter yet.'
'For God's sake gie'z peace o' ma banes!'
The last was his plea when our demands grew too much for him.

8

Peace to his bones!

For six hundred years at least, writers have been making a literary language out of the varied Anglo-Saxon dialects spoken north of the Border. But the 'Scotch' of my grandfather — not very far removed from the dialects of Newcastle, Carlisle and Ballymena — is kept alive by family tradition on the tongues of the people, though it may suffer dilution and change through modern influences and through the fading of many of the old ways to which it referred.

It thrives most strongly in the country places where sheep are still *yowes, tipps, gimmers* and *hoggs* — and *bull* still rhymes with *skull*; where a cow is a *coo* and a herd of cows, *kye*. It prospers also among working folk in the cities when they speak among themselves, though they may be just as ready with Americanisms and Cockney expressions, picked up mainly nowadays from the 'tranny' and the 'telly'.

'OK, hen! If Ah dinnae see ye through the week Ah'll see ye through the windae.'

'Whit? Are ye gonny clean yer windae?'

'Nane o' yer wisecracks, noo!'

It is a far cry from John Barbour in the fourteenth century writing of the heroic deeds of King Robert the Bruce:

> 'And of England the mychty king
> Purvayit him on so great array,
> That, certis, never I heard yet say
> That Inglis men mair aparaile
> Made than they did then for battaile;'

or Henry the Minstrel in the fifteenth century praising 'Schir William Wallace':

> 'Wallace stature of greatness, and of hicht,
> Was jugit thus, be discretioun of richt,
> That saw him baith disembill and in weid:
> Nine quarteris large he was in lenth indeed...'

Yet obviously it is the same old tongue, which was brought into Scotland by the Angles already settled in Northumbria.

Our writers in those days recognised it as 'Inglis', until Gavin Douglas, translator of *The Aeneid*, who lived from 1475 to 1522, began to call it 'Scottis', using 'Sudroun' (Southern) for the Midland dialect of Chaucer whom all the Scottish poets read and admired:

'And yet forsooth I set my busy pain
As that I couth, to make it braid and plain,
Kepand nae Sudroun bot our own langage,
And speakis as I lernit when I was page,
Nor yet sa clean all Sudroun I refuse
Bot some word I pronounce as nychtbour dois.'

A lot of water has flower under Brig o' Doon since then, but many people — and not all of them Scots — still take a delight in resurrecting the old tongue, which, like Charles II, takes 'an unconscionable time a-dying'.

The latest to join the experts in what is variously called 'Lallans', 'Braid Scots' and 'the Doric' is Prince Charles, who recently toured a factory in the Borders where they process vegetables, and joked to the girls that he was wearing a tin hat to protect his head from falling 'neeps'. As an old pupil of Gordonstoun, he naturally knew the Scots word for turnips. I have no doubt he is as fluent in Scots as in the Welsh he took the trouble to learn for his induction speech at Caernarvon.

Even the Pakistani greengrocers in Edinburgh have learned not only to speak Scots to their customers, but even to use it in their ticket-writing. In one Asian window I read 'Nice sproots' and 'Nice West Lothian tatties'.

My grandfather's advice to confine ourselves to words understood by the person addressed is illustrated by the story which has been going the rounds as a result of the plethora of elections we have been having in Scotland. One of our new electors, a pretty eighteen-year-old, dutifully wiggled her way to vote in the Referendum on the Scotland Act, the General Election and then the historic poll on 7 June 1979, for the European Parliament. An inveterate chatter-up of lassies recognized her by her undulations, her blue corduroys, her 'yellie wellies' and the 'wee dug' she had on the leash, then exclaimed: 'Is that you again, hen — exercisin' yer franchise?'

'Naw,' she laughed behind her screen of curls, 'it's no a franchise — it's a chihuahua.'

Scots is a pretty language when it is spoken by pretty people.

Like the Prince of Wales, some of our eight European representatives speak the vernacular when among their compatriots, though they can turn on easily translatable English for international consumption.

'What is the Scots for "Common Agricultural Policy?" ' an enthusiast for the language was challenged.

'What is the English for it?' he retorted.

'Is that you again, hen — exercisin' yer franchise?'

The hornie golach's an awsome beast, soople an' scaly

You would hardly think that such an insignificant creature as the earwig would be regarded in high esteem by the erudite members of the School of Scottish Studies at Edinburgh University. The fact is that the earwig figures bravely in the 'linguistic map of Scotland', as the scholars call it.

This wiggly wee craitrie goes under many aliases. While in Glasgow it is simply an 'eariewig' (and this has nothing to do with the human ear, but refers to the ear of corn or barley in which our Anglo-Saxon forebears believed the insect to make its 'wick' or dwelling), in Edinburgh it is a 'clipshear'.

This East Coast name comes from 'clip' (what a hairdresser does) and 'shears' (the usual Scots word for any type of scissors, and not only for large ones such as garden shears). Edinburgh folk took 'clipshears' to be a plural, and lopped the *s* off the end to make it singular. But more usually they refer to the wee creepie-crawlie as a 'clippie'.

Just to add to the confusion, they use the same word for a wee 'clipcloots', a wifie with a sharp and overworked tongue. Also, they used to apply it to a bus conductress because she clipped the tickets in her machine.

I have even heard it applied to a man. This was a conductor we had on the No. 41 bus which runs right through the city from the hills in the south, near Craiglockhart, to Barnton, near Cramond Brig and the Firth of Forth. He was always cracking jokes and so someone nicknamed him 'the clippie wi' the quippie'.

Almost invariably, however, 'clippie' meant the female of the species. Now, alas, with so many of the Capital's buses being operated by driver alone, 'clippies', with or without 'quippies', are ceasing to be the main entertainment on city transport.

But the other 'clippies', such fun when you find them wriggling out of your salad, are still going strong under their many Scottish names.

Although you will hear them called 'clipshears' in St Boswells, Bowden, Liddesdale and other parts between Edinburgh and the Border with England, most of these Southern Counties have their own names for this quaint little garden pest. These Border names are usually variations of the North of England dialect word, 'twitchbell'.

In Liddesdale the earwig is a 'switchbell' and in some parts of

Roxburghshire it is a 'touchspale'. But in other parts of that county you may hear 'codgebell', with local forms — 'codgybel' or 'codgie' in St Boswells and 'coachbill' in Bowden.

Hawick earwigs, just to be different (a Border characteristic), are 'scodgies', and along the road in Kelso they are 'scodgebells'. 'Scotchbolt' and 'scotchie' are other forms, the Scots appearing to feel they have some affinity with this harassed but indomitable insect.

Now the interesting thing is that, when you cross the Forth into Fife, the earwig becomes a 'gowlack', and as you proceed north and west you find a variety of similar names, from 'golach' to 'gallacher'. All these names are reminders that at one time the Gaelic language had more than a footing in these parts of Scotland, though it has receded and given place to the Lowland Scots tongue in more recent centuries.

'Gowlack', 'golach', 'gaylock' and so on are all corruptions of a Gaelic word *gabhalach*, which means 'forked', and which is applied equally to the earwig, with its 'forceps' at its tail, and the swallow, which has a forked tail. 'Forkie' and 'forkietail' are other names for the earwig which you will find in Scotland. 'Chipshears' also refers to these 'forceps'.

One of the difficulties confronting poets and novelists using Scots is that words have different forms and different shades of meaning in different parts of the country.

As an Edinburgh man I called the gutter running along between sidewalk and carriageway ('atween the plainstanes and the caussay') simply the 'gutter'. But when I began to work in Glasgow I found it was called the 'syver'. This puzzled me at first, because in Edinburgh 'syver' means the drain at the end of the gutter, what the Aberdonian calls a 'brander'. But this drain in Glasgow is called the 'stank'.

Now the only 'stank' in Edinburgh is the 'burn' (brook) which runs through Murrayfield near the International Rugby field on its way nto the Water of Leith. 'Stank' usually means a stream in Scotland, and Burns wrote 'I never drank the Muse's stank, Castalia's burn an' a' that.'

If you cross the Forth, whether by boat or by one of the bridges, you leave one dialect behind in Edinburgh and find a fairly different one over in the Kingdom of Fife.

Across that wee streak of water the 'duke' (duck) of Lothian becomes a 'juck'.

A 'chookie' (hen) becomes a 'chuckie'. That was the form used by Burns, who called Edinburgh 'Auld chuckie Reekie', comparing the

Capital to a broody fowl.

The 'dowgs' (dogs) of the Lothian countryside, more usually 'dugs' in Edinburgh, as in Glasgow, become 'doags' in Fife.

'Yin', the usual word for 'one' south of Forth and Clyde, becomes 'ane' north of that line. In Edinburgh we say 'twae' for 'two' and 'whae' for 'who', and that is the pronunciation in the Eastern Borders, corresponding to the 'whe' of the 'Geordies' around Newcastle. There is, in fact, no abrupt change of dialect at the Border: the dialects of Northern England, Eastern and Western, shade gradually into those of Scotland.

The 'twae' and 'whae' of Lothian become 'twa' and 'wha' in the West, as well as north of the Forth.

An 'eemick' (ant) of Edinburgh becomes an 'emmickie' in Fife, and a 'lympit' (limpet) becomes a 'lempick'.

These variations explain how Scots from different parts sometimes start comparing notes: 'It's funny, in't it, that you say "fesh" whun Ah say "fush".' Both happen to be discussing *fish*.

A Scot asked his crony: 'Hoo did ye git oan in Lunnon, Cherlie?'

'Och,' the other replied, 'no aw that weel. Thae Coackneys couldnae unnerstaun me fur ma awccent.'

'Yet awccent? Whit in the name o' guidness are ye daein wi an awccent, an' you been in Scoa'lan' aw yer life?'

But we do notice one another's accents, and especially differences in intonation. When I was taken through from Edinburgh to Glasgow as a child, an old Glasgow wife, hearing me speak, called to a friend: 'Oh, c'meer an' listen tae the wee Embruh wain! C'meer tae ye hear the wee singsang!'

Young as I was, I was highly amused by this, as I was convinced it was the Glasgow folk who had a 'singsang'. Many years later, when I was working in Glasgow, I called on a commercial traveller named Blackwood, who had been a schoolmate of mine in Edinburgh. As he was absent I left word for him with a Glasgow colleague. This man was unable to wait until my friend returned to the office, but left a note:

> 'A man called Mackie, who sings like a Blackie,
> Called to see you when you were out.'

The implication was that Mr Blackwood and I both had that telltale Auld Reekie 'singsang'. 'Blackie' is also Scots for blackbird.

Glasgow sentences go down the scale, and I suppose ours ascend the gamut. How could I possibly have an accent, and me an Edinburgh man?

14

Whichever brand of Scots we speak, it is usually expressive. One old Scot, sitting on the sidelines at a society ball, was asked what he thought of the ladies' fashions.

'Ah'm damned if Ah ken,' he replied. 'Are thae dames *inside* thae goons, tryin tae git *oot*, or are they *ootside*, tryin tae git *in*?'

'Ah'm that hert-hungry,' said another veteran, 'Ah could eat the Deil (Devil) an' sup his mither.'

'Awa tae Freuchie!' is one of our polite ways of telling someone to go to Hell, but one also hears: 'Ye can gang tae Hecklebirnie if ye like — an' that's three miles past Hell!'

Hell is a real place to old Scots brought up on the so-called 'Shorter Catechism,' a longer document than the C. of E. one. 'Hecklebirnie' suggests a pile of thorns, but 'Go to Halifax!' is commoner, and it raises an interesting point. Apparently Halifax was an American concentration camp in which Scots Colonists who remained loyal to the British Crown in the American Revolution were imprisoned. In Gaelic the Devil is sometimes referred to as *Righ Ealafacs* — the King of Halifax.

Theology is not so much the obsession of the Scots as it used to be. A drunk man at a wedding kept pestering the minister with questions on abstruse religious problems.

'Tell me, meenister,' he asked, 'whit dae ye think o' predestination?'

'Come to me when you're sober,' said the minister, severely, 'and I'll tell you.'

'Ach, when Ah'm sober,' spat the man in disgust, 'when Ah'm sober, Ah dinnae gie a damn aboot predestination.'

A thoughtful little Scot went up to another preacher at the end of service and commented: 'That wiz an intristin sermon ye gied us, meenister, aboot the Judgment Day. Did Ah unnerstaun ye tae say that, when Gabriel toots on his hoarn, awbody that's ivver been in the warld'll be gethert thegither in the wan place at the wan time?'

'Of course,' said the minister.

'Will Cain an' Abel be there?'

'Naturally.'

'An' Dauvit an' Goliath?'

'Of course.'

'An' aw the Cel'ic an' Rangers supporters, an' aw the Herts and Hibs supporters?'

'Indubitably — every man-jack of them.'

'Weel, if that's sae, meenister, ye kin tak it fae me there'll no be

'A *damned* poor show fur Paisley.'

muckle judgin dune the first day.'

A drunk Paisley 'buddie', making his way home through a cemetery became so sleepy that he lay down in the nearest newly-dug grave. As dawn broke, he was awakened by a bugle-call from an adjacent Army camp. Dutifully, finding himself in the grave, he stood up, but as he looked around the cemetery he discovered he was the only one there. He exclaimed:

'A damned poor show fur Paisley.'

You an' mey'll gang an' pow a pey

If we inhabitants of Auld Reekie fail to detect a lilt in our own speech, we notice it clearly enough in the talk of our near neighbours in Lothian and the Borders.

Only three miles away from Princes Street we catch it in the speech of the Portobello folk. 'Porty' (a salubrious seaside resort originally called Figgate Whins, but given its foreign name by a sailor who served under Admiral Vernon in the victory of Puerto Bello) has been part of Edinburgh for well over half a century, but its accents still sound rustic to our city ears.

Sir Harry Lauder, the world-renowned Scotch comedian, was born in Bridge Street off Portobello High Street. So was the mother of Dave Willis, the half-Welsh Glasgow comic whom Sir Charles Chaplin (who had played in vaudeville with Lauder) called 'the funniest Scotchman I ever saw on the stage'.

Dave used to say: 'Ah'm hauf Welsh, hauf Porty, and a hunner per cent daft.'

'Porty' must have been blessed by the god of mirth, for it was the training ground of many Scotch comedians in its pierrot days. Tommy Morgan and Tommy Yorke — and Ike Freedman, the kilted Jewish comedian — entertained in the seaside shows there, where Donald Peers ('In a shady nook by a babbling brook') was the best-known vocalist.

Ike Freedman used to exploit the icy East Coast winds by announcing: 'A little song entitled: "Why do they call me a Jew, when I'm one of God's Frozen People?" '

Lauder's most famous lines occurred in his song, 'A Wee Doch an' Doris' (Gaelic *deoch an doruis*, a drink at the door, or stirrup-cup, taken on leaving a party):

'If ye can say "It's a braw bricht minlicht nicht,"
Then ye're a' richt, ye ken.'

His tongue-twister — meaning 'It's a fine bright moonlight night' — was, like 'The Leith police dismisseth us', a test of sobriety, and, although the comedian spent parts of his youth in Arbroath and Hamilton, the tongue he sang in was still that of Portobello. The only thing he added for stage purposes was an exaggerated rolling of the *r*.

Even more 'landwart' or countrified to our ears is the speech of the Dalkeith folk, six miles south-east in Midlothian. Its bright boys came to school with me at Broughton in Edinburgh, and, although they were grammar-school boys, they retained their 'guid Scots tongues'.

I remember a dialogue between two of them in our science lab, where a group of us were 'scavanglin' or, as we should say now, 'skyving', during a free period. One of these boys came in and took a drink from one of the taps in the lab, using one of the glass beakers which we had for chemistry.

A townie and close friend, whom he had ignored on the way in, asked him if he had forgotten that the Dalkeith fair was being held on the following day.

The boy at the tap asked: 'Are *oo* (we) gaun there?'

His associate, probably affronted at the use of 'oo', which was not included in the dialect of Edinburgh, retorted contemptuously: 'Oo! Oo! Ye muckle soo! It's no a beaker ye should be drinkin oot o' — it's a troch (trough).'

A bout of fisticuffs followed, for no one accepts the epithet 'soo' (sow), even from a townsman and bosom friend. The lad who had used the fighting words grew up to be a leading Scottish surgeon, professor and belted knight, and the one who had said 'oo' for 'we' became headmaster of a school in his native burgh.

Both 'oo' and 'soo' occur in dialects south of the Border. So does the word 'coo' for a cow. There was the historic use of it by George Stephenson, of the 'Rocket' locomotive and the Stockton-Darlington Railway. When he was asked what would happen if a cow strayed on to the line, Stephenson is recorded as saying it would be so much the worse for the 'coo'.

I heard the word 'soo' in the Fylde district of Lancashire used by a well-known local poet and entertainer, Jack Benson, author of *The Eccleston Bull*. When I remarked to Jack that we in Scotland also said 'soo' and 'coo', he told me 'But we don't say "coo" here.'

I could have told him that there were places in Scotland where they don't say 'coo' either, though their dialect otherwise is broad. This is in the Border country where Rugby is the favourite form of football, and where they not only say 'cow' but also 'yow' for 'you' and 'pow' for 'poo' (pull).

In Teviotdale and Liddesdale (central and south Roxburghshire), 'A cup of tea for you and me' becomes 'A cup o' tey for yow an' mey', and 'Yow an' mey'll gang an' pow a pey' means 'You and I will go and pull a pea.' As well as 'oo' you will hear 'wey' for 'we' in those parts. In Liddesdale you even hear 'hool', 'hoorn' and 'nooze' for 'hole', 'horn' and 'nose'.

'Watch oot, or ye'll git yin in the nooze!'

The people who make these weird vowel sounds are usually hefty backs or speedy forwards with whom it is unwise to trifle. Or they are opinionative Rugby *followers*, like the one who cried out to a forceful player brought down by someone heftier than himself: 'That's been a lang time comin' tae ye, mun, and yow's nivver been better served.'

Eastern Border dialects shade into those of North-Eastern England, and those of the Western Borders into the speech of Cumbria. I remember my first taste of the Gallovidian dialect in Wigtown, where a lassie invited me to join her in a walk 'oop the coot' (up the cut — a favourite local stroll). As we were 'dauberin' along, a bird flew overhead and I asked her what it was.

'It's a Muchrum scurt,' she replied without hesitation.

She meant a green shag — what we call a 'scart' in Lothian. Why she assumed it belonged to another part of the coast — Mochrum — I shall never know.

The path we were walking on she called a 'pud'. I had heard paths called 'pads' nearer my home, but it seemed that in Wigtown the *a*s became *u*s and the *u*s were pronounced almost as in Lancashire. When I suggested this to her, she told me I was talking through my 'hut'.

Borderers are as good at stories as at Rugby. One of their provosts used to tell of the Texas oil man who strayed into one of those towns in a break from his exploration in the North Sea. He asked some locals where he could get a shave, and they sent him to the only barber in town — the blacksmith.

This worthy told him to sit on the anvil, fished a bit of carbolic soap out of the iron shavings on the floor, rescued the razor from among the old horse-shoes, spat on the brush and proceeded to make a lather. He went on to give the Texan — a brave man surely — a close shave.

After he had finished, the Texan commented, 'I guess that was all right, but tell me — do you always spit on the brush to make a lather?'

...the only barber in town — the blacksmith.

'Aw, michty mey, naw,' said the smith, 'that's jist fur strangers — if ye had been yin o' the men frae here Ah wid hae sput in yer face.'

The Texan took to this honest man, and pretty soon he was telling him Texan yarns, impressing him with the size of the state he came from: 'A guy can git into a train in Texas at dawn and twenny-four hours later he's still in Texas.'

'Ay,' said the village blacksmith, 'is it no awfy? *Oo've* got trains jist aboot as slow as that in Scotland.'

They talk down there about the district council that is considering putting traffic signals on a certain bad crossing. 'They hivnae ordered the lichts, but they've decided on the colours.'

I imagine the enthusiasm for Rugby stems from the essential tribalism of the Borderers, who are extremely territorial in their enthusiasm. The men of Hawick proclaim: 'Haa'ick's queen o' aw the Borders', though Dumfries claims to be 'Queen o' the Sooth' and has a Soccer team of that name.

The Hawick folk call themselves 'Teries' from their battle-cry, 'Teribus ye Teriodin', which is said to mean, in Old English, 'Thor keep us, both Thor and Odin,' and rhymes sadly with the disastrous Battle of Flodden — worse than anything that ever happened to Scotland at Twickenham, Murrayfield, Wembley or Hampden Park. A lot of the local ritual in the Borders has to do with Flodden, where the 'Flooers o' the Forest were aw wede away.'

At Selkirk the casting of the colours symbolizes the dramatic way in which the tragic losses of Flodden Field were conveyed to the townsfolk. Hawick, Dumfries, Selkirk, Lauder — all have their riding of the marches — and there are other Beltane celebrations in Peebles, West Linton, Melrose, Lanark, Langholm, and Innerleithen — every old town asserting its individuality, like every Borderer. Galashiels has its Braw Lads' Gathering, celebrated in the song, 'Braw lads o' Gala Water.' (Incidentally, 'water', meaning a stream, is as often as not pronounced 'waiter' in the Borders, not 'watter' or 'waa'er' as in some other parts of Scotland.)

It was in one of these Border towns, where everyone knows everyone else, that the minister found out one of his parishioners was having an affair with another parishioner's wife. He said from the pulpit: 'I will mention no names, but if the offender will put a pound in the collection, nothing more will be said of this distressing matter.'

When he was counting the collection he found five £1 notes, and a fifty-pence piece with a note tied round it, reading: 'This is all I've got with me, minister, but I'll fetch you the rest next Sunday.'

the 'twang'.

'There nae that mony strangers comes here,' cracked my cousin Sandy. 'Gin ye think ye see somebody ye dinna ken, it turns oot tae be een o' the neebors wi' a gumbile.'

It was somewhere in the North East that an English hiker came to a farm and thought he would ask for a drink of fresh milk, which he regarded as a real treat. The farmer's wife saw him coming as she worked at the kitchen sink, and she hastened out to greet him. He made his request, and she was only too willing to oblige. She went into the kitchen and came out with the milk in a little bowl.

The Englishman accepted it thankfully and was enjoying it thoroughly when he noticed a little pig trotting over. As it nuzzled his leg, he decided it was not dangerous and proceeded to finish the milk. The pig peered up at him and rubbed itself against him.

'That's a real friendly little pig,' he commented.

'Oo ay!' laughed the wifie, 'she kens her bowelie (recognizes her bowl).'

Sir John Findlay of Aberlour (his estate was next to Kininvie) taught his sons, who followed him as directors of *The Scotsman*, this classic sentence in Banffshire Doric: 'Thur a place caad the Buck o' the Cabrach, far it dang on sax ooks conteenwal, and neer devaald.' It meant: 'There is a place called the Buck of the Cabrach, where it rained cats and dogs for six weeks in a row, and never abated.'

Although, to an occasional visitor like me, it sounded as if all North-East folk spoke alike, the locals knew better. As in Lothian and the Borders, and other regions, there were differences every few miles. My father told me that while he, as a boy, had said 'father' (never 'faither' as in Central Scotland) and 'mither' (mother), the boys on the nearby sea coast — at Buckie, for instance — said 'fadder' and 'mudder'. While he said 'shoother' for 'shoulder', and Buckie boys said 'shooder'.

It reminds me of the two Glasgow men who tried to strike up conversation with a hefty 'Teuchter' (Highlander) in a North Argyll pub.

The Highlander refused to fraternize, having probably heard discouraging stories about 'Glesca keelies'.

'Ah think mebbe he diznae fancy us because we huvnae goat the heederum-hodderum,' one of the Glaswegians told his pal.

'Aw right, Wull,' said the other: 'you *hodd*erum an' Ah'll *heed*erum.'

Do I have to explain that 'heederum-hodderum' means bagpipe music (and, in this case, the Gaelic language).

They had nae whisky, sae they catched nae fish

I am sure my grandfather, William Mackie, gamekeeper of Kininvie, was the original of the story of the gillie who was asked how he had got on with a certain fishing party and replied: 'They had nae whisky, sae I took them far there wiz nae fish.'

My reason for attributing this classic remark to him is that my father told me that, as a boy, he had asked a similar question and received a not very different answer.

Meeting his father coming home from a fishing expedition with visitors to Kininvie, my father asked him: 'Did ye catch onything?'

'Na,' said the old man: 'Ah didnae care for that beggars.' Either the strangers 'didna hae nae whisky, sae they catched nae fish', or they failed to pay the proper respect to my grandfather, who could be very touchy, like most of these proud folk in the North-East.

This was experienced by my Uncle George, the postmaster of Dingwall, whose hobby was painting in oils. He painted two portraits of his father, one showing the old man sitting on the bank of a river, with rod in hand and a book of home-made flies on the grass beside him; the other, a full face.

The model did not object to the fishing picture which was in profile, but he objected to the full face, because he happened to have banged into something and knocked his imperial Roman nose slightly askew. Uncle George was a painfully accurate painter (if he painted a salmon every spot was of the correct hue and in the exact place, and the fish was pretty high before he completed the brushwork), and so he recorded my grandfather's proboscis as one of the facts of life, as plain as the nose on his face.

Now there were two things those old Donsiders could take in liberal quantities — whisky and umbrage. This time the old man took his due of the latter, and said: 'That's nae ma nose.'

Uncle George protested: 'Oh yes, father, it *is*.'

'Ye'll paint it straicht, or ye'll nivver see me nae neen in Dingwall again.'

And he pulled his 'gamey's' tweed hat, stuck with fishing flies, down over his shaggy brows, and walked out of the house.

On another recorded occasion, he was strolling in the country with two of his sons, and they stopped for tea at a cottage, where the wifie regaled them with home-made scones and fresh 'kirn' butter. The

27

'That's nae ma nose!'

only thing she omitted to give them was 'birse tea,' that is, the tee-total beverage 'wi a cinder in't' (laced with whisky).

When she had presented them with the bill (and I cannot imagine how infinitesimal it must have been compared with our modern prices) and was in the kitchen looking for change, the old man brought a red handkerchief, with white spots, out of his pocket and wrapped what was left of the butter in it.

The sons eyed one another with amusement, but the father declared: 'We've damped-weel peyed for't.'

My grandfather's mortal enemy in Kininvie was a poacher called 'Dirt Jock' because, hating gamekeepers and gillies, he went round at night smearing filth on their door-handles just to let them know what he thought of them.

Now it happened that my father, as a loon, wandered into Elgin one day and saw in the window of an antique shop an old flint-lock pistol of the type sometimes picked up at Culloden and other Jacobite battlefields. Happening to have made some money doing odd jobs around the estate, he managed to buy the gun and acquire instructions on its use, and the powder to fire in it.

He took his treasure up into the heather at Kininvie and, hidden in a whinbush, experimented with loading it. Having packed it with powder and wadding, he closed his eyes, held it high in the air away from him, and pulled the trigger. The noise of the shot echoed round the hills and my father felt like the culprit of the Appin murder.

It was only then that he noticed that his father and Munro the gardener had been a few yards below him, cutting rushes. They would not have seen him, hidden as he was in the bush, but in any case they did not wait to look in the direction of the shot but ran off as fast as their feet could carry them.

My father, stricken with guilt, dug a hole and hid the weapon, then sneaked home. It was hours before my grandfather arrived, puffing, blowing and perspiring as if he had never ceased running.

He fixed my father with a wild glare, and the loon waited in trepidation for the axe to fall. But what the old man said was 'Did ye see Dirt Jock?'

'Na, father,' his son replied in relief. 'Nivver nae hint nor hair o' him.'

'The blackgaird!' swore my grandfather. 'Ah'll get him yet. He fired a shot richt under my bliddy neb, and Ah've been scoorin the countryside for him.'

Late in life, he went with my father to Alford, where he had been

29

born — to be precise, in Tough, pronounced 'Tooch'. He had not been in the district for many years, and hardly knew a soul there, but persisted in greeting everyone with 'Ay, ay, mun!'

'Fa's *at* (Who's that)?' my father would ask.

'*Him?* Oh, that's Joahnnie Achindachie, him that's mairried on een o that Shands.'

His pride would not permit him to acknowledge that he had not the foggiest notion who the man was, but for every passer-by he was able to invent a name and a genealogy.

Another of his pretences was that he not only recognized individual sheep, but even bees flying past or hovering about blooms at the side of a lane.

'That's een o mine,' he would declare, and he would turn to the bee and croon: 'Awa hame, mun! It's weerin late.'

'Is *that* een o yours, father?' his son would ask, just to test him.

'As a maitter o fack, it's nae,' he would reply. 'It's een o the aul wifie's at the back o the squeel-hoose (school-house) at Maggieknock-ater.'

On what was probably his one and only visit to Edinburgh, he swore that Dr Crippen, for whom there was a hue-and-cry out at the time on suspicion of murder, had tried to pick his pocket when he was looking at a fruit cart in the High Street. 'Ah wid ken him ony place: he had a richt hangdog look, jist like Dirt Jock.'

When my father joined the Regular Army (this was in Queen Victoria's time, years before the South African War), the old man disapproved. 'They're nae nithing in the sodgers but rogues an' thiefs an' vaigybones.' But he was proud when his son came home in kilt and white spatterdashes, and showed him around as if he were 'Fechtin Mac' himself.

The Buchan countryfolk are a hard-headed and very opinionative race. They judge people by what they are contributing to the economy.

When I was camping with Sandy Donald in a farm field outside of Keith, I discovered that, with charcoal from the fire, I could decorate the exterior of the tent with bold drawings. I did one of my boyhood hero, Charlie Chaplin. The burly farmer came along just as I had completed the cartoon.

'Charlie Chaplin!' he said, but before I could congratulate myself on the likeness, he spat in disgust and added: 'He maks his livin ackin the goat.' Having settled that, he turned on his heel and walked away.

As for the traditional 'Aiberdeen joke,' there is a lot of truth in the

30

local comment: 'Ach, we jist mak them up oorsels.' It was Aberdonians who fed the *Punch* artist, Charles Keene, with the ideas for his cartoons about 'gruppie' (mean) Scots.

My own favourite is of the Aberdonian who was on a visit to Edinburgh and stood at the Register House under the equestrian statue of Wellington ('the Iron Duke in bronze by Steel'), admiring Princes Street. A perfect stranger came up to him and asked if he had a match.

The Aberdonian produced a box he had just bought in Woolworth's and the stranger, taking it from him, said: 'You are a very lucky man. I am on a campaign advertizing these matches, and I am pleased to inform you that you have just won a pound.'

Without more ado, he pressed a crisp pound note into the Northerner's hand and bustled off.

The Aberdonian looked for a moment at the prize, then came to his senses, and shouted after the man:

'Hi, come back! I kent there wiz a swick in't. Ye're awa wi ma matches.'

Matches, or as we call them, 'spunks', figure in another tale, of the Northerner who had to change trains at Perth. While he was there he went to the station bookstall and bought a box of matches. When he tried to light up his pipe, however, he found that the match would not ignite.

He went back to the bookstall and told the assistant: 'This spunks'll nae scart.'

'What d'ye mean?' protested the assistant, and, taking the failed match out of the other's fingers, he immediately set it alight by striking it on the seat of his own trousers. He handed it over for the Aberdonian to light his pipe with the good-going flame.

'That's aa verra weel,' commented the customer. 'But gin ye think Ah'm gyann tae come aa the wey til Perth Station ivvery time Ah need tae scart a spunk on yeer dowp, ye hae anither think comin.'

Talking of railways, George Elrick, the Aberdonian band-leader, singer and impresario (once celebrated as the 'smiling voice of radio' and dubbed by me 'Elricktricity'), told me there used to be a station-master on the line north whose call to passengers, as a train pulled in, was: 'Here ye are for far ye're gyann! Ye 'at's in there for oot here, come oot, for this is *it*.'

A train was just starting when an old wifie, laden with parcels, threw herself into a first-class carriage. A porter opened the door and asked, 'Madam, are you first-class?'

'Ah'm fine, thank ye.' she replied. 'Foo's yersel?' And as he gave up and shut the door, and the train got away, she turned to another passenger and said fervently: 'Sic a ceevil craitur!'

Two loons on an Aberdeen bus noticed a fine-looking girl stepping on. One said, 'D'ye nae ken her? She's the nicest quyne in Mannofield.'

'Ah've nae doot ava,' said the other, but added in a whisper: 'Aa the same, dinna lat on ye've seen her till she's peyed her fare!'

An old Aberdeenshire farmer had been married more than once and each time his wife had brought him a substantial 'tocher' (dowry). A friend commented: 'Ye'll be makkin a bit o siller oot o this.'

'Ooh, Ah dinna ken. Be the time ye tak them up and pit them doon, there nae that muckle left.'

They say a local football 'Derby' suffered a long delay in starting. They couldna find the penny they tossed up.

Ye vratch, ye've vrutten that aa vrang

Many of the tales of the North-East concern a character called Feel Jeemie Fleeman (the fool James Fleming). He was supported by a Laird of Udny for his amusement, but, although, as they used to say, 'ninepence in the shilling', had a way of surprising people by his sagacity.

When someone asked him whose fool he was, he replied: 'Ah'm Udny's feel: faaz feel are ee (Whose fool are *you*)?'

Sitting on a wall, gazing at a horse-shoe he had picked up, he was told by a smart passer-by: 'Ay, Jeemie, 'at's a horse-shae.'

He replied: 'Min, ye're a smert chiel: foo div ye ken it's nae a meer's (mare's) shae?'

Someone else, to mock him, asked him to spell 'Rotten Slough'. He made what I have always thought was a brilliant stab at it: 'Err oh etten-otten slee oh ech-ech.'

He was only one of many characters of whom tales abound in Aberdeenshire and Banffshire. There was Dr George Hay, the physician of Auld Keith, who died in 1814 at the age of 105 after a life of popularity as an 'original'. He was well known for his velvet cap and his odd sayings.

'Weel,' he asked one patient, 'fit news the day?'

'Oh, very bad,' he was told. 'The French have gained a great victory and the English have sustained much loss.'

'Weel, ye see,' commented the doctor, 'they winna lat them be.'

That just about sums up the whole business of warfare.

He had his own words for everything. A pinch of snuff was 'a dry dram' and crutches were 'oxter staves' ('oxter' is almost the universal word for 'armpit' in Scotland.)

To a man with a large family he said: 'Odd, mun. Ah winner ye dinna think shame. Ah, ah, siccan a muckle faimily — een, twa, three, fowr, sax, aicht — ay, a hale fisher dizzen! Ah, fie, fie for an aul man! Ye'll nae live tae see the youngest keep a chap aff its ain heid.'

Keith had another legendary doctor — William Dougall, who died about the beginning of last century. He initiated his own health service by making the rich and pretentious pay for the poor. One patient kept reminding him she was 'the gweedwife o Boat o Brig', so he 'chairged her the meen (moon)', and told his poor patients later: 'Dinna fash yersel! 'At's aa richt! The gweedwife o Boat o Brig settled yer accoont.'

He could be short with some of his wifies; for instance, the one in Boharm whom he told to take a tablespoonful of a certain medicine so many times a day. She kept asking him, 'Is't a *tea*-speenfy, doctor?'

'Nae a tea-speenfy, dammit,' he roared: 'a table-speenfy, a brose-speenfy, a pothitch-speenfy, ye clod-heidid bitch!'

To a wifie from Bodenfinnoch, who arrived 'in a cowp cairt', he had a testy answer.

She said: 'Ah winner fit maks ma een (eyes) sae weak in the mornins.'

'It's jist because they're in a weak place.'

A poor young mother came to him with a problem. How could she cure her child of her habit of stuffing her toes into her mouth?

Said Dr Dougall: 'Lassie, the little een is deein fit ye canna dee yersel — she's makkin baith ends meet.'

He advised another patient to suck an orange after swallowing castor oil, and then added the warning: 'Dinna fling the peelins on the fleer, in case, gittin up in a hurry, ye gyang an' pit yer fit on them an' faa an' brek yer hoch an' gie me a sax-ooks (six-weeks) job o ye.'

To a wifie complaining she had not 'sleepit a wink for twa nichts,' he advised: 'Ye've great need tae be thankfy that ye get a dover in the daytime, for plenty fowk dizna get that.'

'Doctor,' said the henwife on the market day, 'hiv ye an yntment for ma man's beldie heid?'

'Na, na! Tell yer gweedman he's jist barfit (barefoot) on the croon.'

'Doctor,' said another 'deemie', 'Ah suffer a great deal wi ma een (eyes).'

'Ah dinna doot it, but ye'd suffer a great deal mair withoot them.'

'Doctor, doctor, Ah've been trevvlin the fleer (walking the floor) the hale nicht wi the sair teeth.'

'Weel, seein ye hinna made muckle be the fleer, try the reef (roof) the nicht.'

'Ye micht gie me something for't.'

'Ah, the Deil's in yer heid — better a teem hoose (an empty house) nor an ill tenant.'

'Wid ye gie me a cure for a sair heid?'

'The Keeng's Croon winna cure his sair heid.'

Another woman asked, 'Fit am Ah tae dee wi ma heid?'

'Weel,' he said, 'it's nae great thing o a heid, but ye mun jist keep yer ee on't.'

He told a boy to shoot out his tongue, and then commented: 'Laddie, ye've a tongue as lang's yer mither's.'

'Ah'm oot o ma jigement wi ma teeth,' said another wifie; 'poo them aa!'

'Na, na! ye're nae aul eneuch yet tae be hen-moothed.'

'Fit's vrang wi ye noo, Mrs Watt?' he asked another.

'Stoons (sharp pains) in ma heid.'

'Ye ocht tae be thankfy there somethin in yer heid.'

A gassy beggar-wife said to him: 'The ae half o' the worl dizna ken foo the ither half lives.'

Dr Dougall replied: 'Aweel, it's nae *yeer* faat if they dinna.'

To another woman he said: 'Ah hear the meenister has been catecheezin ye.'

'Ay, he wiz that — spierin an' spierin' (asking and asking); he spiert fit Ah wiz composed o.'

'Oh? An' fit did ye say til that?'

'Ah said we wiz aa fearfully and winnerfy made.'

'Huh, tell him fan he spiers at ye again that an umman is composed o twa hunner an' forty-three beens (bones), a hunner an' saxty-nine muscles an' three hunner an' saxty-nine peens. Ye'll bleck the meenister. Tell him tae back-spier ye there!'

'Foo's yer grandmither the day, Nelly?'

'Some better.'

'Ye'll better tak care o her, for ye winna get anither,'

'Doctor,' said yet another woman patient, 'hae a look at ma tongue an' tell me fit it needs.'

'Rest!' he retorted briefly.

It is not only in that airt that 'sair' (sore) is an overworked word. In many parts of Scotland we say 'sair teeth', 'sair heid', 'sair wame' for toothache, headache and stomach-ache. But 'sair' has many more uses.

'Ay, mun, it's a sair fecht.' (A hard struggle.)

'Ma een's sair.' (I have sore eyes.)

'He wiz aye a sair maister.' (A hard taskmaster.)

'Ye dinnae ken hoo sair wrocht (hard-worked) Ah am in this joab.'

'It's sair wark, Ah tell ee.'

'Thoan wiz a sair shoor.' (A heavy downpour.)

'Ah dinna like the look o'm — he's sair altert.' (Much changed.)

It is often used for 'very'.

'Ah'm sair sweir tae dae't, aw the same.' (Very reluctant.)

'He wiz aye a sair thocht tae me.' (A terrible worry.)

Another characteristic of what Dr William Grant, in his extremely useful introduction to *Chambers' Scots Dictionary*, calls 'Mid North Lowland,' is the pronounciation of the *w*, which we keep silent, in words such as *wretch* and *written*.

'Ye vratch, ye've vrutten it aa vrang.' (You wretch, you've written it all wrong.)

Our silent *w* there becomes pronounced as a *v* — quite a Continental touch. But then there are many affinities between the speech of the North of Scotland and of Flanders, the Netherlands, Germany and the Scandinavian countries. The coming and going of many peoples across the North Sea — mostly of Germanic race — has had a marked influence on the language, as on the type of people you find up there.

Here are other peculiarities. Words such as 'bone', 'stone' and 'one' become 'been', 'steen' and 'een.' A lawyer becomes a 'lavyer' (I often heard my father pronounce it thus). 'Naked' becomes 'n'yackit' and 'going', 'g'yaan'. 'Far ye gyaan?' (Where are you going?) 'Good' becomes 'tweed' and 'school', 'squeel'.

My father used to imitate the stentorian tones with which one farmer would speak to another, from one end of Mid Street to the other, in the days before microphones and loud speakers. He called it a 'stage whisper'.

'Ay, Joahnnie, foo are ye?'

'Fine, Mattie, fine. Foo'z yersel?'

'Ooh, nae bad, nae bad. Foo'z yer neeps?' (How are your turnips.)
'Nae bad, nae bad. Fit aboot yer barley?'

So it would go on, a nice quiet, friendly conversation over their primitive telecommunications.

Two such farmers were elders of the same kirk and, as they farmed far apart, they met only on Sundays, when their strict Sabbatarianism forbade business transactions. This kind of conversation arose in the kirkyaird:

'Did Ah hear ye wiz sellin yer young grey meer?'

'Mebby ye did. Gin this wiz Monday Ah'd hiv socht ye up tae see her an' we could hae haen a dram.'

'Ah ken the meer weel. Gin this wiz Monday Ah'd hiv been spierin fit ye wiz seeking for her.'

'Min, if it had been Monday Ah'd hiv been askin forty pound.'

'If this wiz Monday Ah'd hiv offert ye thirty.'

'Weel, gin this wiz Monday, jist tae settle it, Ah'd hiv suggestit spleetin the deefference.'

'Jist that than! Ah'll send oor Dod up wi the forty the morn, an' ye can gie him the meer's bridle as a luck-penny. Ye ken fine we canna dee business the day!'

My father fascinated my children with his almost French pronounciation of the letter *i*. He always said 'poseetion' and 'Keeng.' This after many years away from Banffshire.

He himself was amused at an Aberdeen loon in Edinburgh commenting on another lad's skill at whistling.

'Min, ye're a gran fussler. Faa learnt ye tae fussle?'

Ay, up there it's not 'Speak Scotch or whistle!' but 'Speak the Doaric, or fussle!'

36

The pure shilder huz nae shairs

If there is such a thing as Standard Scots, apart from the attempts of us writers in *Lallans*, *Akros*, *Lines Review* and *Chapman* to spell the words as nearly alike as possible, the closest approach to it in actual dialect is Sir James Wilson's *Lowland Scotch, as Spoken in the Lower Strathearn District of Perthshire.*

Sir James, himself a native of that district (around Crieff, famous for its Hydro), issued his monumental work in February 1915, forty years after Sir James Murray's *Account of the Dialects of the Southern Counties of Scotland*, in which the hope was expressed that a complete dictionary of the Northern variety of English speech would be compiled, and that, by way of preparation for such a dictionary, a worker in each district would record the local pronounciation of all the words used in his dialect.

'Much has been done in this direction by the publication of Professor Wright's *English Dialect Dictionary*, but the ground covered by that work is so wide that it is difficult to extract from it general information regarding any particular dialect or group of dialects; and the Scottish Branch of the English Association is now engaged in collecting materials for a new Scotch Dictionary, which will give a complete account of all the dialects now spoken in the Lowland parts of Scotland.'

Since then we have had much useful work, in the *Scottish National Dictionary* itself, *Chambers' Scottish Dictionary*, Nicol Jarvie's *Lallans* and William Graham's *Scots Word Book*. Sir James confined his inquiries to the dialect spoken in the valley of the River Earn, in the South-East of Perthshire, between the Grampians and the Ochil Hills, 'which forms part of the tract called by Sir James Murray "The Highland Border" and is included in the area defined by Professor Wright as "North Middle Scotland".'

Sir James's book is still highly valued by scholars and should be read by all who are seriously interested in spoken Scots, though it is unlikely that even in Strathearn the dialect has stayed put since 1915. I happened to work — and loaf — in that same district in the 1920s, however, and found the local speech little changed. My drinking companions among the budgies in the Star Hotel, Crieff, spoke pretty much as Sir James Wilson had recorded little over a decade earlier.

Now, just about that time, a man from Langholm, partly educated in Edinburgh, called Christopher Murray Grieve, had adopted the pen-name of 'Hugh MacDiarmid' and begun to write poems in Scots, which later became famous. Dr Grieve died recently at the age of 85, having established a world reputation as a poet in both Scots and English.

The interesting thing is that the inspiration for his first famous lyric in Scots, *The Watergae* (indistinct rainbow), came from the lists of words which Sir James Wilson had collected from those old characters in Strathearn.

Sir James, who went in for phonetic spelling, recorded the word as 'waatur-gaw'. His 'authorities', old whiskered worthies looking like actors in *Bunty Pulls the Strings* and *The Bonnie Brier Bush*, still called the sky the 'luft' (the same word as we get in the title of the German airline, Lufthansa). To them a windy day was a 'fine reevin day' ('reevin' means stealing, so I suppose it was a day when the wind would steal the clothes off the line).

Summer lightning was 'wuldfire'; for 'frost in the air today' they said: 'Thur a nup ee air the-day.' A heavy shower was a 'doon-richt poor'.

Actually, most of their words are still to be heard in Perthshire, but nowadays, when somebody says 'watergaw', it is 'a bubblyjock til a wee bantin hen' that he or she got it out of the poems of MacDiarmid, just as 'a daimen-icker in a thrave' (a spare ear in a collection of sheaves) betrays the reader of Robert Burns.

This same poem of MacDiarmid's contains the word 'yowe-trummle' (trembling of ewes), and there it is, right above 'watergaw,' on page 169 of Wilson's book, defined as 'cold weather in July after shearing'.

MacDiarmid's most memorable line in that epoch-making lyric, 'There was nae reek in the laverock's hoose', occurs on page 190 of Wilson's book under 'Proverbs and Sayings'. In his phonetic spelling it is given as 'Dhur'z nay reek ee laivruk's hoos dhe-nikht.' (There's no smoke in the lark's house tonight: said when the night is cold and stormy.)

That poem, inspired by brilliant dialect fieldwork in Perthshire, working on the vivid imagination of a young ex-Serviceman born almost in the North of England but proudly Caledonian in his enthusiasms, was the beginning of what a Frenchman, Dr Denis Saurat, called 'the Scots Renaissance'.

The language around Crieff is not only geographically 'Central Scottish' but it also presents a kind of average of the language. (The term 'Lowland Scotch' is used to denote the dialects *outside* of Gaelic, which is a Scottish dialect of the Irish language and thus quite distinct from 'Lallans'.

I have always felt that 'Lowland' is a bit misleading in its geographical use in Scotland, for large swatches of the so-called Lowlands are by no means low, and linguistically these dialects stretch far up into what we call 'the Highlands'.

They spread right up the centre of Scotland and rub shoulders with Gaelic in Perthshire, and right up the East Coast into the North Sea fringe of Ross and Cromarty, Sutherland and Caithness. West of this coastal fringe there are Gaelic speakers, or, where Gaelic has receded, you find a preference for good English.

This is perhaps the origin of the saying: 'The best English in Britain is spoken in Inverness.' Now, it is true that many Invernesians speak very careful English, but in that town, as in most urban areas of Scotland, you will find a lot of rather slovenly language, too.

North of the so-called 'Highland Line' is where the Lowland dialects acquire that *f* for *wh* in words such as 'fa' (who), 'fan' (when), 'far' (where), 'fat' or 'fit' (what), 'faaz' (whose) and 'fither' (whither). Approaching Aberdeen about Stonehaven we are hearing them say 'meen' for moon, and 'steel' for stool.

My brother George used to call this 'speakin Keith'. As the train stopped at one of those stations on the way north, and we heard the people on the platform through the open carriage window, he would tell us, 'There's some folk speakin Keith!'

There are many odd sounds on the way. What we call 'a sair wame' (stomach ache) in the South becomes 'a sair wime', they 'wive' cloth instead of weaving it and they declare: 'Man, that's grite (great)!'

By the time we get to Caithness, the *f* for *wh* has disappeared and where the Keith folk were saying 'gweed' (good) and 'queet' (*cuit*, ankle), the locals are saying 'geed' and 'keet'. As I sat in a pub in Halkirk, I thought at first the old cronies there were talking either Norwegian or Gaelic, but eventually I understood it as just another kind of Scots. One of the experts on Caithness dialect is the poet and playwright, Donald Campbell, who is a 'Wicker', though resident in Edinburgh.

Caithness folk do not roll the *r* like most Lowlanders, but curl their tongues backwards over it like some Gaelic-speakers. This is rather attractive, especially in lassies.

They also say 'mure' and 'pure' for moor and poor (in Lothian we say 'mair' and 'pair', and in the West it is 'merr' and 'perr').

Most oddly of all, a chair is a 'shair' and children are 'shilder'. So if you hear 'The pure shilder huz nae shairs', you know the neglected bairns just have to sit on the 'fleer'.

These Northerners, like some Glaswegians, tend to drop the *th* (a bothersome sound to Glasgow folk, too) in 'the', 'they', 'that' and 'there'. There is a Gaelic touch in such words as 'wifag' (wifie), 'bairnag' (bairnie) and 'lempad' (limpet).

It was a Wick man who said: 'Aa yer geese isna swaans — some o them's white elephants.'

The old wife who was suspected of having a lot of treasure laid away, and not in the bank, was described as having 'An in-ablow-a-bedfu o aathing ye can think o.'

Was it a man from Caithness who found himself in the First World War (the Great War, as we called it) in Mesopotamia, and heard someone say that that was the site of the Garden of Eden?

'If 'at's' a case,' he declared: 'if issiz' a Gairden o Eden, nae winner 'a Twelve Apostles got 'ursels flung oot o't.'

Wick folk, like Aberdonians, react strongly against South of Scotland attempts at standardizing Scots. They did not like the Lyon Court's motto for the town, "Wick Warks Wonders". They said it should be 'Wick *Wurks* Wonders'. Actually he would be a clever heraldic limner who could spell it the way the Wickers say it.

From somewhere up there comes the classical Crofter's Prayer: 'O Lord God of Battles, stretch forth thy hand, we beseech Thee, over oor Wullie, who, as Thou art aware, is a sodger in the Seaforth Highlanders fechtin in France. Protect him from all the perils o' the battlefield and bring him hame safe efter a victorious peace. And O Lord, Thou whose paths are in the deep watters, stretch forth Thy protecting hand over oor John, a leading seaman in the *Royal Sovereign*; guard him from all the perils of the sea and guide him hame in safiety unto the harbour where he would be. An' then, Lord, 'ur's wee Davie — ach, Lord, nivver fash yer thoom owre wee Davie! He's here at hame wi us an' we can look efter him wursels.'

Azzizzattat? Hannie's or Enderetta's?

Lopping the beginnings off words is common in many dialects and Dr William Grant noted it particularly in parts of the Black Isle, where the *wh*, which we saw suffering some indignities in Angus, Kincardineshire and Aberdeenshire, is dropped altogether in 'who', 'what', 'where' and so on. So we get such weird sentences as:

'Ah Sammy deet?' (Who saw me doing it?)

'Attabotzat?' (What boat is that?)

'Azzizzatbot?' (Whose is that boat?)

'Atteenwuzzit?' (Which one was it?)

The Black Isle is part of Ross and Cromarty, said to have obtained its name through remaining dark in colour when other parts were white with snow. My wife's folk were Frasers and Bains from that airt. It is another of those odd parts of the Northern East Coast where Anglo-Saxon came in conflict with Gaelic and Norse, and apparently came away with a few bruises.

In Scotland we pretend that the dropping of *h* at the beginnings of words and putting it in where it ought not to be, is something purely English, and characteristic especially of Cockneys. In fact all of us tend to drop the *h* in some instances in rapid speech, but in the Black Isle there are folk who vie with the Cockney in swapping the *h* around — the tendency of which Professor ''Ennery 'Iggins' spent so much time on trying to cure 'Helizer' Doolittle. Yes, in the Black Isle there are worthies who say: 'Atz up wi yer ahn?' (What's up with your hand?) 'Kin ye no add it be the esp?' (Can you not hold it by the hasp?)

To compensate, they stick the *h* on to 'egg', calling it 'a hegg', and can say, 'Wull ye hae some hile (ale) or wid ye rether hae a hegg or a happle?'

A boathook becomes a 'botuck.'

Up there, 'Azzattizzat? Hannie's or Enderetta's?' means 'Whose hat is that — Annie's or Henrietta's?' I am sure the costers of 'Ammersmith would get on well with these Black Isle folk. Was it not a Cockney who asked, 'Wot'll I do about me 'eadache?' and was advised, 'Try a haspirate!'? That could almost be a Black Isle story.

Words such as 'pear', 'swear', 'tear', 'shame' are pronounced almost in a London fashion — 'pire', 'swire', 'shime', and one hears 'hime' for 'home', 'bine' for 'bone', and 'stine' for 'stone' — all as in German.

Fishing villages around the Moray Firth have such odd pronunciations, and suggest that the fishing communities may have been of different origin from their neighbours.

Sir James Wilson, in another of his books, *The Dialects of Central Scotland*, drew attention to the difference between the dialect of the fishing village of Newhaven in Edinburgh and that of the surrounding area. Strangely enough, the old fishermen he consulted in the 'Newhaven Parliament', a shelter near the harbour, said 'Wales' for 'whales', just as a Cockney — or indeed many English speakers — might.

Newhaven folk used to be renowned for referring to their near-neighbours to the east as 'foreigners fae Leith', and there is no doubt that the fishing village, recently attractively refurbished, still has a distinctive look, and its old inhabitants still have the air of belonging to a community of their own. The same may be said of the folk of Fisherrow, the fishing section of Musselburgh, East Lothian.

Years ago, I went to Newhaven Fish Market in the very early morning to do a piece for the *Scottish Sunday Express*. I met a bunch of Fisherrow wifies in their traditional costume and with their creels, for they still bought fish in the market and sold it round the doors with their creels on their backs and the straps over their brows.

Interviewing them, I sought their names and addresses to give the touch of authenticity to my report. This aroused the suspicion of one typical fishwife, who stepped back out of the crowd and eyed me up and down as cannily as a herring gull.

Eventually she stepped forward and 'spiered richt oot at me':

'*Whit* paper did ye say ye wiz fae?'

'*The Scottish Sunday Express*,' I replied.

'Aw ken ye noo!' she exclaimed, as if she had caught me with my hand in her creel. 'Ye wiz at me yince afore ettlin tae geet me tae buy that paper.'

She had me confused with the men who used to go round the doors trying to build up the circulation of their periodicals.

It was down in Newhaven Fish Market that one of the 'unctioneers' emphasized the freshness of the fish he was selling with the cry: 'Lookit that noo! Is that no fresh? Guidness me, *terra firma* huznae set in yet.' (He was no doubt thinking of *rigor mortis*, but to a fish salesman one swatch of Latin is as good as another.)

One of his rivals picked up the phrase and, not long after, was heard declaring: 'Here a richt fresh shot o' fish. *Terra cotta* huznae set in yet.'

'...foreigners fae Leith...'

It was a Newhaven man who courted a Leith lass with chocolates every Saturday. After they had married, she looked in vain for these tokens of love. When she complained, he retorted: 'Lassie, there's nae yizz baitin the heuk efter ye've landit the fish.'

A tourist, talking to a lobster fisherman at Crail Harbour in Fife, watched him bait his creels with fish and asked: 'Do you think that bait's good?'

The Crail man said: 'Na, Ah dinnae, but the lobsters dae.'

'Queer fowk, the fisher fowk' is a saying among inland people up north, who are conscious that the fishers are a race apart. The sea-coast dwellers have the same feeling about the landwart folk. On the other hand, in the 'crofter counties' the tradition has been to combine fishing with land work. Nowadays, too, the men on the trawlers are not so exclusively drawn from the coastal communities. The motor car has broken up a lot of the tribalism, in Scotland as elsewhere.

The old fishwives used to be able to put their creels on the front of the trams beside the drivers, but the switch to buses deprived them of that privilege and they took to bringing their creels to town in taxis. Lately the coast folk have concentrated on selling round the doors from vans.

A Port Seton fishmonger selling in an Edinburgh suburb heard a woman customer complain she did not like the looks of any of the fish in his van. He retorted: 'Gin it's looks ye're efter, missiz, ye should buy yersel a goldfish.'

'Are your fish fresh?' another suburban lady enquired.

'Whit d'ye mean "fresh"?' asked the salesman. 'Dae ye no see the beggars'll no lie doon?'

Of a persistent critic of his fish, a fishmonger from the coast commented: 'Ach, that wife's like a flet fish: her mooth's nivver straicht.'

In my boyhood the fishmongers' call, as they sold from floats drawn by ponies, was 'Caller haddie!' (fresh haddock), a cry I often heard from Peter Victory, father of the Scotch comedian, the late Johnnie Victory. Peter pronounced it 'Cullahuddie!'

'Caller' is familiar to most people from the song 'Caller Herring', often sung by the Newhaven Fishwives Choir.

'Caller Herring' has been traditionally the tune associated with the old Glasgow Corporation, although the song is about the Firth of Forth. It may be something to do with the fact that a red herring was known as 'a Glasgow magistrate'. But it was this conjunction that inspired the parody:

'We are Glasgow Bailies,
You read about us in the dailies,
Handsome Glasgow Bailies
Reared on banks of Clyde.

'When we are mairchin' in procession,
Wi' dignity an' grave discretion,
Ye can tell frae oor expression
We believe in slow progression.

'We are Glasgow Bailies,
Ye'll fin us whaur the guid Scotch kail is:
Brae big Glasgow Bailies,
Kent baith faur an' — wide.

'We're honest Glasgow Bailies,
Captious critics may assail iz:
Wha but Glasgow Bailies
Could be sae deegnified?

'We're stalwart Glasgow Bailies:
Wi' muckle banquets they regale iz:
In their toasts they rise an' hail iz
As the city's pride.

'If in the street ye sing a chorus,
For breach o' peace ye're hauled afore iz;
Nivver on yer knees implore iz,
Tears an' daft excuses bore iz.

'We are Glasgow Bailies
An' we kin show ye whaur the jail is:
Lea' it tae the Bailies
Justice tae decide.

'Up in George Square we sit debatin,'
Solemnly deliberatin',
Fur tae keep on legislatin',
Universal bliss creatin'.

'We are Glasgow Bailies,
Oor coaminsense will nivver fail is;
Wark on ony scale is
Taen jist in oor stride.

'Sae trust the Glasgow Bailies,
Whit though o' drift the coamin tale is;
Lea it tae the Bailies,
The Ship o' State tae guide.

'For we are Glasgow Bailies,
An hard-up folk fur handoots trail iz,
We're as rerr as caipercailies,
Truest sons o' Clyde...

'Glasgow Bai-lees! Glasgow Bai-lees!'

Alas, that municipal reorganisation did away with the figure of the
Glasgow Bailie or Magistrate! A Justice of the Peace is no substitute.

Whaar da Viking cam hiking, look oot fir gruliks

A Shetland editor visiting me in Edinburgh said: 'It's the first time
I've been in Scotland since before the war.'

I had to adjust my mind to the fact that he was talking of 'crossing
to Scotland' from the Northern Isles, for to both Shetlanders and
Orcadians 'Mainland' means their own largest islands, and Scotland is
another country.

Vikings took over these islands and populated them with Norsemen.
It was seven hundred years later that the Scots recolonized them. As a
result the Northern Islanders speak 'Insular', a mixture of Scots and
Norse (or, as they call it up there, 'Norn'). Both Orkney and Shetland
have Norn dictionaries.

The New Shetlander encouraged writing in the local dialects, but
the leading Orcadian writers, such as Edwin Muir and George Mackay
Brown, seem to have felt their dialect was too obscure for the outside
world — including Scotland — and have preferred to write in
excellent English.

46

My favourite Shetland poet — the late T. A. Robertson ('Vaga-land') — produced a Shetland grammar. 'God faa dee!' (God bless thee!) is an example of his foreign-sounding language. Addressing the small animals which come out at night as 'peerie (little) folk', he writes: 'Dey're plain tae be seen ida aze o da car-lichts.' (They are plainly to be seen in the blaze of the car lights.) Here are a few of his words and phrases:

'Aa God's mak', all God's creation.

'Alamootie', the stormy petrel.

'Baa brakkin', sea breaking on a sunken rock.

'Banks-flooer', the sea-pink.

'Blinkie', an electric torch.

'Blugga-flooers', marsh-marigolds.

'Blue joob', the deep sea. Also 'da far haaf'.

'Brimmastyooch', spindrift.

'Dadderie', drudgery.

'Dratsie', the otter.

'Get a firsmo', be taken down a peg.

'Gloy', straw for making a 'kishie', a basket for carrying 'paets' (peats).

'Grottie', covered with oily sediment — a word that, spelt with a 'y', has spread much further afield than the Shetlands.

'Klashmelt', a mess.

'Kokkilurie', the daisy.

'No a hirnik o da kin', not a single relative.

'Perskeet', fastidious.

'Ragnarok', the end of the world.

'Rivin o da dim', daybreak.

Many of his words are recognizably Scots, such as 'trunsher' for a large plate, 'trok' for trade and 'whalp' for pup, but others, such as 'yarta' for sweetheart and 'haaf' for the open sea, take us into another world. Their deep-sea fishers are known as the 'haaf men'.

For 'this', 'that', 'they', 'them', the Shetlanders say 'dis', 'dat', 'dey', 'dem', and we get 'strent' for strength and 'lent' for length, 'tink' for think and 'tree' for three. 'Tak a shance, Sharlotte!' means 'Take a chance, Charlotte!'

Orcadians say 'Chon' for John and ask: 'Are ye enchoyin' yerselfs?' Their greeting is 'Ay, man, it's aaful weet!' or, if you are lucky, 'Ay, man, it's a grand day!' and if you ask permission to do something, they say: 'Deu that sam!' (Just you *do* that!)

In Shetland you have to look out for 'gruliks' (masqueraders) and 'skeklers' (Halloween entertainers), and listen to tales about 'trows' (trolls) and 'peerie folk' with such names as 'Peesterleetie', 'Terrie Mittens' or 'Trunsher Face'. Orcadians also have contact with the 'peerie' or 'peedie' folk and have an 'aaful' bother with 'hogboons' (mound-dwellers).

There are persistent stories in the isles about 'selkies' (seal-folk) marrying humans, usually with ultimately tragic separations through the call of the deep. The well-known and very beautiful folk-song 'Silkie' tells one version of these stories. Orcadians believe some things are 'grotti' (lucky), but this does not include a minister aboard, who is as much of a menace as Jonah.

Witches used to sell favourable winds at 6d each, and a fair breeze might cost as much as 1s 6d. I have no record of the tariff in inflation times.

The Orkney hogboons, like the broonies of more southern parts, would do household chores unbidden, appreciated food left for them but were easily insulted by the wrong gifts — for instance, clothes. One hogboon was offended by an Orkney farmer's wife and became such a pest that the farmer decided to move. He made his way to his new home with his goods, including a churn ('kirn'), on his pony's back, and as he was completing the journey, commented: 'Weel, praise the Lord we're quit o' that pest!'

The words were scarcely out of his mouth before the hogboon stuck his head out of the churn and declared: 'Man, we're gettin' a grand night for the flittin'!'

Now the hogboons and trows are back in the shape of oilmen but no doubt the gruliks and skeklers and Eynhallow guisers and 'Up-Helly-Aa!' revellers will take care of them.

There are many stories of Orcadian farmers. One of them, who was a seafaring man, was troubled for years with rats, with which his place was overrun. Then suddenly the rats disappeared. Now the old salt, remembering about rats leaving a sinking ship, was worried in case the same thing applied to a farm. To his relief the rats eventually reappeared, but he still worried about the cause of their absence for a period. Then he recalled that one of the lads had been trying to learn the concertina. The rats had not returned until the lad had given up and sold the 'squeezebox.'

Another Orkney farmer got everyone down with his constant grumbling, especially about his poor returns from his outlay on the land.

One year he had the best crop in all Orkney, but as friends came

'Up-Helly-Aa' revellers will take care of them...

round and congratulated him, all he could say was 'Mebbe ay, but damn it, man, look at the pooer it's takin' oot o' the grund!'

The folk tales of the Northern Isles are rich and gripping — they include a Cinderella tale in which the heroine is Essypattle (Scots 'ashypet' has the same meaning as Cinderella); legends about a 'Lost Atlantis' called 'Hether Blether' which some 'haaf men' have claimed to see; Hildaland, the land of the Fin Folk (a mysterious people sometimes confused with the Finns); and a Jack in the Beanstalk tale. 'Finfolkaheem' (the Finfolk's home) is the Orkney version of Lost Atlantis. Indeed, all the universal themes seem to be represented, but with the background of the Isles.

'Eence apon a time' (once upon a time) is the 'aald wife's' favourite opening to a tale to make the bairns' hair stand on end. With traces of prehistoric dwellers — Picts or whatever — around them, and with Norse and probably Gaelic mythology in their cultural background, the Shetlanders and Orcadians can hardly fail to have a sense of other worlds around them, especially in the long winter nights.

But an oilman up there who found himself being followed around by either a trow or a hogboon, got tired of the creature's attentions and eventually turned on it and said: 'Now, buzz off! Otherwise I'll take a couple of aspirins and that'll be the finish of *you*!'

Awra same, ye cannae whack Glesca

My wife enjoys talking to strangers. In a Glasgow nursing-home they would not believe she was an Edinburgh woman. She was 'too friendly'.

This is the persistent myth of the Glaswegians about the Edinburgh people — a cherished myth which one tries to dispel at one's peril.

Glasgow folk like to be told that they are the friendliest people in the world, and Glasgow-based media play up to this. It is no doubt to throw the open-heartedness of the Glaswegians into sharp relief that we of the Capital are almost invariably represented as 'stuck-up' and 'toffee-nosed'.

When I worked in the Second City, they called me a 'Geich'. They called me other things as well, but this is not that kind of book.

I have never found out the origin of the word 'Geich', unless it has some connection with the fact that James IV went round in the disguise of 'The Guidman o' Ballengeich,' in the play about his encounter with Jock Howieson of Cramond Brig, which was a great favourite in the 'penny geggies.'

Now it is perfectly true that Glaswegians are a hail-fellow-well-met race. They have also a great sense of humour. It is only at — and after — football matches that they tend to lose their sense of humour and their Christian forbearance and love of their neighbours.

My old friend, the Yorkshire comedian, Arthur Clifford Baynes ('Stainless Stephen'), was staying at the Ivanhoe Hotel in Buchanan Street, Glasgow, and went into the residents' lounge for a drink on his way to bed after doing his stint at Glasgow Empire. He told me next morning: 'The place was deserted except for one Scotch-man who sat by himself shouting out: "Thur foarty million folk in England an' Ah dinnae gie a damn fur wan o' thum." '

'Stainless' — who became famous on the radio by reading out all the punctuation marks in his script — used to get a relatively good reception at Glasgow Empire, reputedly 'the graveyard of English comedians'. The Empire was equally the graveyard of many a would-be Scotch comic. Even Sir Harry Lauder could 'get the bird' there.

The feeling against Edinburgh is probably stronger than any against England. The recent marathon Scottish Cup final between 'ra boays in blue' (Rangers) and the 'High Bees' or 'Hibs' (Edinburgh Hibernian) finished eventually in a win for the Glasgow side and saved 'No Mean City' from a wave of depression. They feel the Scottish Cup belongs to Glasgow, even though the supremacy of 'the Aul' Firm' (Rangers and Cel'ic) is not keeping the gates from dwindling.

'Wiz it a big gate, china?'

'The biggest Ah've ever climbed owre.'

In the relations between Glasgow and Edinburgh the fighting word is 'Capital'.

'Embruh's mebbe the Capi'al, china, but Glesca's *goat* the capi'al. See aw thae Civil Servants through err — bloa'it boory-crats — wha's subsidizin' um? *Uz!* Ra people o' Glaazga. Mine ye, Ah've nuh-hin agane Embruh. Ah jiss canna staun the bliddy place. Ah like Aiberdeen, Perth, Stirlin, even Dundee, but Embruh — *ach*! Awra same, china, ye huv tae admit it: ye cannae whack Glasca. It's goat sump'n. Eh? Whit's it goat? *Uz!* WE ARRA PEOPLE!'

There is a lot of truth in the claim today, when Glasgow is definitely improving its amenities and its tourist appeal, and when the friendliness of the people, combined with the attention being paid to modernizing the city while retaining its most attractive traditional features, is presenting a real challenge to Edinburgh. The Capital, as the orators of 'No Mean City' ('clitch efter clitch efter clitch') now have the opportunity of intoning, must 'look to her laurels'.

'Let Glasgow flourish by the preaching of the Word' (*Uz*!). It is a better motto than Edinburgh's 'Nisi Dominus frustra'. (Unless ye're a Loard, it's a waste o' time comin here.')

'You must admit Edinburgh is well laid out.'

'Lissen, china, if you were deid as lang as Embruh, you'd be weel laid oot anaw.'

'I say, have you any family?'

'Oo ay, china, Ah've twa brithers livin, an' wan in Embruh.'

Glasgow is a go-ahead city because its citizens are so adaptable. Silicon chips with everything! 'See that compu'er, china? Thoan's a great invention. Thur still a loa' o mistakes, but noo thur no naebody tae blame fur thum!'

Now the average Glaswegian sees much of the world far beyond Merryhill and Brigton, even beyond Rossie Bay, Dunoon and Millport. Costa Brava rivals Costa Clyde. 'Ay, china, costa bliddy foarchin!'

'See me? Ah went on a cruise — naw, no a *booze*, a *cruise* — an' Ah'm sittin foarnent this Frenchman fur aw ma meals — ken? — an' ra first time we sits doon foarnent each urra — ken? — this wee Froggie says "Bawn appy tea!"'

'Well, see *me*? Ah wiz nivver at nane o yer Glesca High Skills or Hutchie's Grammar — ken? Ah nivver goat nane o this parlyin the bat at the skill. Sae Ah thinks the wee Frog's tellin me his *name*. Sae Ah gies um the noad — ken? — an' says "Sannylanns."'

'At's ma name — ken? — "Sannylanns," spelt wi twa *d*'s.

'Well, nixt time we sits doon foarnent each urra he's at it again: "Bawn appy tea!" an', like a clown, yours truly is answerin um: "Sannylanns."'

"This goes on like a bliddy Princess pantymine. Awra time, awra time, till Ah gits up tae here wi it an' Ah goes tae ra Heid Stewart and Ah tells um:

"See at wee Frog ye pit at ma table? Ivvery time Ah sit doon he tells me his name's 'Bawn appy tea', an' Ah tell um mines is Sannylanns. He nivver gits ra bliddy message. Ah hink he's needing his heid luckt or sump'n."

' "Ach, china," he says (he's wan o *uz*, the Heid Stewart, like, jiss like the Chief Engineer on awra boats), "you're awaw wirra blissit ferries, *you* are," he says. "Rat wee Froggie's no tellin you his *name*, he's sayin 'Here's wishin ye a guid appetite fur yer denner!' See whit Ah mean? 'Bawn appy tea!' means 'Guid appetite, crap fur aw coarn, doon ra blissit hatch, bung ho!' ''

'Well, ye could huv cawed me owre wi a paper hankie. Sae the nixt time the perr o uz is sittin doon foarnent each urra, Ah beats um tae ra bliddy punch. Ah lifts ma gless o ra hard stuff an' Ah fixes um wi ma eye, an' Ah says: "Bawn appy tea!"

'An' ra wee Frog lifts *his* glass o some bliddy fizzy watter and says: "Sannylanns!" Ye cannae bliddy *win, kin* ye?'

My favourite Glaswegian was a 'wee fluh' called Andy Cowan Martin. There were many tiny people in the city in those days — their children are noticeably taller — but Andy was exceptionally short. A journalistic colleague, Clyde Irvine, who had been in the States and talked like Damon Runyon, called him 'That sawn-off guy.'

Andy himself joked about his stature: 'Ah'm suing Glasgow Corporation fur buildin the pavements owre near ma dowp.' When he spoke at a dinner, his head scarcely peeping over the table-top, he would remark: 'Ah'm no still sitting doon. Ah'm staunin in a hole in the grun.'

When he moved through to Edinburgh he fixed a low peg in the Press Club cloakroom so that he could reach it to hang up his coat.

He was editor of the Bridgeton weekly, the *Eastern Standard*, in the Second World War. Those were the days of Press hand-outs by the Ministry of Information, through St Andrew's House. They were cyclostyled and usually bore a 'stop date' with the warning that on no account must the contents be published before a certain date. The reason was partly security and partly the desire to give all the papers an equal chance of coming out with the news.

It happened on one occasion that Andy got the one copy some functionary had forgotten to stamp with the 'stop date' and the warning against premature publication. So the *Eastern Standard* came out before any other paper with the announcement that the Bailey Bridge had been invented and was going to be used by Britain in the war.

There was an immediate hullaballoo. Not only were the bureaucrats annoyed at the leak, but, even more, the editors of the other papers were wild at Andy jumping the gun, and were ringing up St Andrew's House to have the 'wee fluh's' head on the block, or at least to see that he got a 'sherrickin'.

Well, of course, Wee Andy was able to produce his copy and show that, so far as he had been informed, there was no embargo, and he was adjudged innocent and never sent to the Tower.

The following week, the *Eastern Standard* came out with the front-page banner headline: 'The paper that scooped the world.'

It was the *Skibbereen Eagle* all over again ('Let the Tsar of All the Russias beware! The *Skibbereen Eagle* has its eye upon him.')

At an earlier period Andy had worked for the D. C. Thomson newspaper group on the *Sunday Post* and the *Weekly News,* and one of the editors assured me that he was the original of 'Wee Andy, the resourceful Master of Ceremonies of the Okey-Dokey dance hall' in the popular, and very Glaswegian, 'Stories from the Courts' series in the *Weekly Record.*

Another time, Andy found a job as a 'venterlokist's' doll in a variety act. He was as tiny as that.

He worked for me on the *Edinburgh Evening Dispatch* for a spell, but moved out to Guyana — then still British Guiana — where one of his jobs was to conduct a black world champion on a triumphant whistle-stop tour. Andy attracted more attention than Tiger, the stalwart national hero. In the wee Glaswegian's own words, 'Ah stole the show, like the wee dug at the flea circus.'

Before he died, he found his niche as a football commentator on radio, and listeners visualized him as a big deep-chested ex-Rangers back. He had that weight in his voice, and confidence in his delivery.

Now the best-known Andy on the radio is Andy Cameron, another typical Glaswegian, disc jockey on Sunday afternoons, with messages and jokes rolling in from listeners in Nethy Bridge, Barra, Benbecula, Alness and Nigg, indeed from everywhere. His Edinburgh rival is Gerry McKenzie, the Tartan Terror, who enjoins wifies in such quiet little places to 'keep taking their tartan tablets!' A woman's voice every now and then tells us: 'I'm converted to Gerry McKenzie, the Natural Gas mannie on the tartan trannie.'

Gerry also repeats what he calls 'Gerry-atric' jokes sent in by his listeners. Andy Cameron might say: 'There's nothing but strikes just now — the crocuses came out and then the daffodils came out in sympathy;' then Gerry will give us 'Even the bees are coming oot, fur shorter flooers an' mair honey.'

One gets the impression of a whole nation laughing, from Papa Stour to the Mull of Galloway. It goes to prove that there is as much fun in Lochboisdale, Brora and Achiltibuie as in the Big Smoke. As the Lewisman said, after a visit to Glasgow: 'Och, I could haff got chust as *meeshkyach* (drunk) in Stornoway.'

The road and the miles tae Dundee

One of the most popular songs brought back into circulation by the modern folk-song enthusiasm is 'The road and the miles tae Dundee', sung with great effect by that Angus loon, Andy Stewart. The city he celebrates, famed for jute, jam and journalism, stands out on its own dialectally.

Whereas most Scots pronounce 'I' as 'Ah' or, in the Southern Counties, 'Aw', Dundee eccentrically pronounces it 'Eh'.

'Ye ken whit Eh fancy?' a Dundonian might say. 'A peh (a pie).'

'He's a fleh (fly) mick, yoan.'

'Nae wunner! He comes fae Feff (Fife).'

'Eh, man, they weel say, "Eff Ell Weh (F-L-Y) — Feff." '

A friend of mine, Ames Imrie, left Dundee to become City Chamberlain of Edinburgh. Now in Edinburgh there are people (locally nicknamed 'Moaninsaiders' — Morningsiders) who think it posh to pronounce 'I' in this way. So Ames Imrie used to jest, 'When Eh came to Edinburgh speaking Dundee, Eh found Eh was talking posh.'

Apart from turning an ice-cream slider into an 'ess-cream sledder' and a 'byre' (cow-shed) into a 'berr', and claiming that 'the ferr's the best flooer i' the gairden' (the fire's the best flower in the garden), Dundonians speak a vigorous Scots. It was the hinterland of this city that produced the Scots writings of Sir James Barrie, such as *The Window in Thrums, Auld Licht Idylls* and *The Little Minister*. These books are rather sneered at by Scots writers of today, but they are rich in Scottish dialect words.

Barrie has been satirized for his sentimentality, his mysticism and his whimsy. If found myself doing it in the old *Glasgow Evening News* in the Thirties, when Elisabeth Bergner was appearing in the title role of Barrie's *The Boy David*:

A' the road frae Thrums
Wee Jimsy Barrie comes,
Fleein owre the hoose-taps
An' blawin doon the lums.
Wi' a wish ablow ilk oxter
An' kisses roon his thumbs—
Oh Jimsy the Whimsy
An' his wee fairy chums!

There is glamourie an' witchery
An' magic when he flees.
A kilt made oot the stuff o' dreams
He wears aroon his knees.
His belfry's fou o' baukiebirds,
His bonnet's fou o bees—
Oh Jimsy the Whimsy
An' the muckle weird he drees.

There's gnomes ahint the ingleneuk,
There's kelpies in the shed;
There's sprites inside the aumrie
An' elfs ablow the bed;
There's witches on their besom-shanks,
An' through the luft they've spread—
For Jimsy the Whimsy
On honey-dew has fed.

Barrie's 'Thrums' (named after a weaving expression for the fringe of warp threads remaining on a loom beam when the web has been cut off) is his native Kirriemuir in Angus. 'Kailyaird (cabbage-patch) literature' is the label usually tied on to his work by modern critics. He was writing of a rural Scotland which has largely gone, or rather has been much modernized. Hand-loom weaving and horse farming have been replaced by industrial estates and mechanization on the land.

Folk-song, especially the bothy ballads of the North-East, the territory we gradually come into in the hinterland of Dundee, also takes us nostalgically back to the days of the horse plough and harrow, when many farm servants were required and enjoyed the comradeship of the bothies, while complaining about the niggardliness of their employers:

'The breid wiz thick, the brose were thin,
    The broath they were like bree:
Ah chased the barley roon the plate
    An' aa Ah goat wiz three.'

'It wiz that soor it gart me thraw ma moo.' (It was so sour it made me twist my mouth.)
'We rise as seen (soon) as mornin licht,' the singers complained. 'We're warkin life oot tae keep it in.'

The bothy had 'sic a foo stink', such a foul smell, and the 'kitchen deemie' (the lass working in the kitchen) 'wiz a gey clottie worker' (a rather hit-or-miss one).

At the 'plewin (ploughing) match', they said, 'the judges' sicht wiz gey peer' (rather poor).

Even if many of the conditions have altered, the words of these old bothy songs are still readily understood, even by city youths who never ploughed a furrow, straight or squint, but who are caught up in the folk-song revival. And many of the words and phrases are still used by such country folk as survive the latest industrial revolution:

'Fit wiz the skith?' (What was the harm?)

'Ah cannae git a wink o sleep fur loons practyzin that geetars.'

'It winna dee.' (It will not do.)

'He didnae hain his-sel.' (He did not spare himself.)

'Ah fair felt the grun o ma stammick.' (I certainly felt the base of my stomach — I was starving.)

'Ye're far ben wi that quyne.' (You are well in with that girl.)

'It's like fur tae ding on.' (It looks as if it is going to rain.)

'Hain yer sheen, bairns! Leather's dear.' (Preserve your shoes!)

But the bothy ballads sometimes take a 'coorser' view of 'Thrums' than Barrie allowed himself to do. Witness the Rabelaisian song about that same 'toon' — 'The Ball o Kirriemuir' — which was 'X Certificate' enough for our pilots to sing it to one another over the intercom on their way to bomb Hitler's Germany:

> 'Fa'll dee't this time? (Who'll do it this time?)
>> Fa'll dee't noo?
> The een 'at did it last time
>> Canna dee't the noo.'

In the language of the old farmyard, 'bylie', which to us in the cities would convey a bailie or magistrate, means a cow-herd; a sluttish girl is called 'a richt flodge'; when you are knocked up by hard work you are 'fair forfochen'.

At a 'free-an'-easy' in a North-country 'howff' (pub), an inebriated folk singer in a kilt was playing the piano 'side-saddle' in a desultory way, while smoking his cigar and swigging from a pint on top of the instrument. The embers from his cigar fell on his sporran, and that hairy purse began to smoulder and smoke.

He went playing on, obviously not aware that his clothes were catching fire. One of the drinkers got up and went forward to him with the words: 'D'ye ken yer sporran's in a lowe (alight)?'

'Na,' replied the kiltie, 'but jist you sing it an' Ah'll vamp.'

The word 'til' is used for 'to' in many parts of Scotland, including Lothian and Borders. It is used increasingly as one goes north, and in Keith they even say 'tae-til', meaning right up to a place: 'Pit that steel (stool) tae-til the waa (up against the wall)!'

In medieval Scots we get 'He till't and she till't', describing a battle of the sexes. And we still hear 'Pit it tillum!' (Put it to him); 'Herk tiller!' (Listen to her); 'The hoose hizna a reef til't' (The House has no roof to it); 'Ah'd tak a pinch a saut til't' (I'd take a pinch of salt to that).

'Be' or 'by' is often used in comparisons. 'Man, ye're big be me'; '*Oo're* better off be *you*' (We're better off than you); 'He's that blin he disnae ken a hoose be a heystack i' the derknin'; 'He disnae ken a *b* be a bull's fit' (said of someone who cannot read or white).

'As' and 'nor' are both used instead of 'than'. 'Ah grew a sicht bigger as ma big billie' (Rather bigger than my elder brother). 'Better you nor me!' (You can have it!)

'Or' or 'ur' (ere) is used for both 'before' and 'until': 'Jist you wait ur yer paw comes hame an' you'll git it, ma laud!'

Somewhere up north in the course of the Second World War a Home Guard on patrol saw a young couple emerging through a hedge, and challenged the lad:

'D'ye ken ye've been in a prohibitit area?'

Immediately the girl protested: 'Fit d'ye mean? He hiz *not*.'

A farm servant, who was leaving in any case, was asked by the 'kitchen deemie' if his tea was all right.

'Jist richt,' he said.

'Fit d'ye mean — jist richt?'

'Weel, gin it had been ony better Ah widna hae gotten it, and gin it had been ony waur (worse), Ah widnae hae drank it.'

A student was asked by a relative how he was getting on at college.

'Nae bad, nae bad,' he said. (Things are usually 'not bad' in Scotland — we seldom enthuse.)

'Weel, keep the pudden het!' he was told. (Keep it up!)

A slow worker was thus described: 'He's been kens-lang oan that joab.' ('Kens' for 'God kens'.)

'Whan did Joahnnie gang?'

'Och, twa oor syne (two hours ago). He'll be kens-whaur be noo.' (He will be goodness-knows-where by this time.)

We hear a lot about 'tatties' (potatoes), our staple diet. It used to

'D'ye ken ye've been in a prohibitit area?'

59

be 'tatties an' herrin', but now the herring is a scarce and dear commodity. A 'tattie-bogle' is a scarecrow (potato-ghost) but also a child's toy made with match-sticks stuck all over a potato, usually an oddly shaped one. 'He's no the clean tattie' is a common criticism of a doubtful character, but 'tattie' can also mean ragged. Sometimes it is 'tatchie' — 'He wiz a gey tatchie-like buddie.'

'Teekie' was my father's word. He hated to see any of us leave the house looking 'teekie', dishevelled or carelessly dressed. 'Wait till Ah pit a queeff in yer hair!' he would say, producing a comb. The 'queeff' was the smart parting which he had favoured when he was a soldier and still had hair to part.

There is a good word, 'peuchlin', to describe the dilatory worker — 'A peuchlin body that nivver wins aff the bit', but it can also be applied to the weather. A day of continual drizzle is a 'peuchlin' day. Sometimes, 'the snaw's peuchlin oan' or we just get 'a peuchlin o snaw', a steady 'on-ding'.

The most modern phenomenon can be described in good Scots. For instance, a beatnik, or a bearded student, is characterized as 'yin o' thae hairy-oobits wi a heid like a pease-wusp' (one of those hairy caterpillars with a head of hair like a tangle of pease-straw).

Eetle oatle, black boattle, eetle oatle, oot

James Ritchie, the Montgomeries, Amy Stewart Fraser and others have collected the rhymes Scottish children recite or sing when they play with skipping rope or ball, or at hopscotch ('peevers').

'Stoatin the baw' is how bouncing a ball is described in the towns and cities in the Industrial Belt, and the rhymes that go with 'stoatin' or 'stoatie' vary from place to place. They recently inspired a story which went the rounds.

A minister passing along the street stopped to listen to a wee girl playing 'stoatie' and discovered to his horror she was reciting 'The Pakistanis huz aw the hooses'. He said, 'Now, lassie, could you not recite something nicer?'

'Whit'll Ah say?' she asked, innocently.

'Well, for instance,' he suggested, '"Jesus was born in a manger."'

'Aw right, well,' she agreed, and went back to her 'stoatie' with:

'Jeezis wiz boarn in a manger,
Fur the Pakistanis huz aw the hooses.'

Apocryphal, I hope! As I was a laddie, I did not play at many
lassies' games, so I do not remember many of the ball-bouncing, skipping or 'peeverie beds' rhymes. I do remember the counting-out ones
which we employed to decide who was to be 'het' at 'A-Leave-Oy',
the hide-and-seek game in which we could free those who had been
caught and impounded.

'Eetle, oatle, black boattle,
Eetle, oatle, oot.'

'As Ah went doon the London Road,
Ah met a scabbit cuddie,
You one'd it, you two'd it...'

That count went on until 'you *ate* it!' which never failed to give us
boys a wicked laugh.

If the person who was 'het' was reluctant to leave the 'den' and
hunt for us in the stables and other places where we hid, we set up a
chant:

'Come oot yer den,
Ye dirty wee hen,
An' look fur aw yer chickens!'

If the game was stopped for some reason, there was another chant:

'Come oot, come oot, wherever ye are!
The ghemm's jigged up, aw through Joahnnie Paiterson.'

In Glasgow they said: 'The ghemm's jagged', or 'Ra baw's oan the
slates'.

Some of the counting-out rhymes are so ancient they may well have
been originally Anglo-Saxon attempts to imitate the speech of their
predecessors, Welsh-speaking Britons or Picts, or liturgical Latin:

'Eenty, teenty, halligo lum...'

'Eenerty, teenerty, fickerty fay,
Ell, dell, doaminay,
Urkay, burkay, stoorie roack,
Ann, tan, toozie Joack.'

> 'Ease oaz, pease brose,
> Easy-oazy oot.'

I did not mind the rough boys' games, but when the girls sang enticingly:

> 'Whae'll come intae ma wee ring,
> Ma wee ring, ma wee ring?
> Whae'll come intae ma wee ring
> Tae make it a wee bit bigger?'

— I ran several streets away. To be seen 'playin wi the lassies' was to lose one's hard-earned status as 'yin o the laddies'.

> 'Ah took a letter tae ma luv
> An' oan the way Ah droapt it,
> A dree, a dree, Ah droapt it...'

Oh, help! 'Ye widnae see me fur stoor.'
The kinds of rhyme it was not beneath my dignity to learn were:

> 'Dan, Dan, the funny wee man,
>   Washed 'is face in a fryin-pan,
> Pertit 'is hair wi the leg o a chair,
>   Dan, Dan, the funny wee man.'

> 'Hi, Joack, ma cuddie,
>   Ma cuddie's oan the dyke,
> An' if ye middle ma cuddie
>   Ma cuddie'll gie ye a bite.'

> 'Aw, Joahnny Cramond,
>   Ye hink ye're awfy neat,
> Skinnymalinky long legs
>   An' umberellie feet.'

The lassies could *keep* their skipping, 'stoatin' and 'jing-a-ring' rhymes. And I never played 'peevers' in my life. Any contemporary who alleges that will be 'taen up fur sclander'.

Bairns still furnish us with good stories. There is the one about the youngsters who were encouraged to write their own Nativity play and perform it at the Sunday Skill. They made it very modern and realistic. When the couple arrived at the inn, the innkeeper said: 'Heh, yous, ye cannae git in here: the place is full up. Can ye no read the notice in the windae — "Nae vacancies"?'

'Ah, but ma missiz is gonny hae a wain, ony meenit noo.'

'That's no *ma* faut.'

'It's no *ma* faut, well.'

There was the old 'Granda' who was listening to the wifies discussing the new bairn.

'He's goat his mither's een aw richt.'

'Mebbe ay, but he's goat his faither's moo.'

'Izzat so?' chipped in the old man. 'Weel, this mornin the wee beggar had *ma teeth.*'

The wee boy asked the teacher, 'Please, miss, kin a laddie be beltit fur something he huznae din?'

'Of course not.'

'Ah huvnae din ma hame lessons, well.'

'What's wrong with Tommy's composition?' a teacher asked.

The 'neighbour' replied: 'Please, miss, he's went an' pitten "pitten" whaur he shouldy pitten "pit"!'

'Pitten' is the old past participle of 'put', just like 'gotten' which is good Scots as well as good American.

A small boy, accompanied by his even smaller sister, was asked by a kindly old gent: 'How many are there in your family?'

The laddie replied: 'Thur five o *uz* — an' wan o *her.*'

A mother pestered by the over-activity of her pre-school boy asked him irritably: 'Kin ye no fin something tae dae, laddie?'

He gave the classic reply: 'Hoo kin Ah dae ocht whan there's nocht tae dae ocht *wi*?'

Our favourite game as boys was a rough one we called 'Cuddie Wechts', in which one boy stood with his back to the wall and another stood bent forward with his head in the first boy's stomach; then we all tried to pile on to the second boy's back. Those who fell off formed a chain on to the second boy, and others tried to see how far forward they could leapfrog. I believe in New York it is known as 'Johnnie on a Pony', and in Scottish towns it goes under various names, from 'Hunch, Cuddie, Hunch' to 'Bab at the Bowster'. 'Cuddie Wechts', by the way, means 'horse (or donkey) weights', and 'Bowster' means a bolster.

Memorizing the Books of the Bible, we used to recite:

Matthew, Mark, Luke and John,
Hud (hold) the cuddie ur (till) Ah git on.'

We used to ask raw boys: 'Huv ye ivver seen a *green dug*?' — 'dug' being the way we pronounced 'dog' in the city. Usually the victim said: 'Naw, Ah've nivver,' and we would say, triumphantly: 'Well, *Ah* huv. Ah saw ma faither diggin the public green.'

'Bizzim' used to be our favourite word for miscalling a girl, in the days before permissiveness in language. The girl had a standard retort:

> 'A bizzim's a broom
> Fur sweepin a room,
> An' Ah'm a lady's daughter.'

Looking back, I realize my repertoire of children's rhymes and songs was not an extensive one. However, I knew most of the Halloween and Hogmanay guisers' rhymes, with which we hoped to win handouts, usually at the downstairs (servants') doors of big Georgian houses in the New Town of Edinburgh.

> 'Tramp, tramp, tramp, the boys are marching,
> We are the guisers at the door,
> If ye dinnae let us in, we will bash yer door in,
> An' ye'll nivver see the guisers any more.'

> 'Please tae help the guisers, the guisers, the guisers,
> Please tae help the guisers an' Ah'll sing ye a bonnie wee song;
> New Year's comin, the pigs are gettin fat,
> Please tae pit a penny in the auld man's hat.
> If ye huvna goat a penny, a ha'p'ny will do,
> If ye huvnae got a ha'p'ny, God bless you!'

We did not know, and have not learned since, what on earth 'Hogmanay' meant. I cannot believe it is from the French, '*Au guy menez*', which is said to mean 'Lead to the mistletoe', with, I suppose, some phoney Druidic significance. I prefer the Danish scholar's suggestion that 'Hogmanay, trollolay' is of Scandinavian origin and related to those 'hogboons' of Orkney and 'trows' of Shetland: 'Hogman, hae! Trolls away!' or words to that effect.

The guiser's song, sung in Shetland on Old New Year's Eve, is called 'Da Huggeranonie Sang', and the gruliks (masqueraders) there appear to be engaged in banishing the 'trows'. Huggeranonie is apparently a 'trow's' name (probably from the Norse, *haugr*, a mound from which the hogmen or hogboons emerged).

64

The way my mother took care to clear the house of old rubbish and ashes before the New Year came in, and the welcome given to the First-Foot, who had to be dark, and a male, to bring luck, suggests the tie-up with getting rid of the old 'trows' of the past year, and all the bad luck they had brought with them, and welcoming in a new 'hogboon' in the hope he would bring better fortune in the ensuring year.

If '*Au guy menez*' is Norman French — also '*homme est né: trois rois là,*' another suggested derivation — we must not forget the Normans were originally Norsemen, and might have adapted their old phrases to French when they got themselves new helmets.

A personal confession: I have never 'first-fittit' any house in my life, unless inadvertently. The reason is that I am bad luck. I was born a redhead. And the bairns' rhyme which haunts me is:

'Go hame tae yer dinner,
Ye rid-heidit sinner,
Yer mither wants carrots fur stew.'

She wid gie kens-whit fur a man

Women's Lib — or 'Weemen's Leeb', as they call it in the North — gets little support from the Scottish language. It is a first-class tongue for 'miscawin fowk', and especially for putting the 'deemies' in their place.

Scotsmen are not only male chauvinist pigs. They are 'handrackle' (inconsiderate), 'mad keen on fitbaw', 'branksome' (strutting), 'hungry brosers' (big eaters, making unconscionable demands on their unpaid 'skivvies' and 'scudgies'), 'lazy hanyels aboot the hoose', 'contrairisome', 'gruppie', 'tentie o their siller fur theirsels', 'keelies an' rannieguls' in their treatment of their wives, 'funkies' to their bosses but not to their domestic slaves, not very often 'joco' (amorous) except to other women, 'aye blowstin' (always bragging) and 'awfy scowfs' (terrible blusterers).

They think their wives are 'whaup-nebbit' (long-nosed like curlews — in other words, inquisitive), 'aye nebbin' (always nagging), 'forrit-some' (not knowing their place), too often 'peenjie' (fretful), not sufficiently 'tholemudie' (patient), 'aye ahin wi the hoosewark', with a tendency to 'gittin things aye erse-forrit' (getting their 'pri*ror*ities

…'Ah wiz married til 'ur…'

wrang'), 'glaikit' (stupid), 'Toarn-faced like a loorie luft' (like a cloudy sky), and, of course, terrible 'fagmafuffs', 'gush-pots', 'hash-magundies' and 'country clypes' (the number of synonyms for 'gossip' is endless).

Fortunately the women have their great gift of patience, which they define as 'byde a wee and dinna fash yersel!' When that deserts them, they have plenty of ready-made repartee:

'Nane o yer beak, ye big cleck!'

'Ach, dinnae think ye're the big billiedackus!'

'Dinnae come the tin man wi me, ye dyke-lowpin skipe!'

If more eloquent words evade them they can always make do with:

'Awaw'n bile yer heid!'

'Ach, dicht yer neb an' flee up!'

'Awaw'n caw yer girr or doze yer peerie!' (Away and trundle your hoop or spin your top!)

Most of us, despite the high place given to men in the Scottish family social scale, get the worst of it when we try conclusions with 'ra wife'.

How we ever acquired our status to begin with is a mystery, for tradition has it that we are, as the modern phrase expresses it, 'lousy lovers'.

As we invented 'gowff', I suppose it must have been a Scot who interrupted his putt to remove his cap and stand erect as a funeral passed near the golf-course. His opponent remarked: 'Ah didnae ken ye wiz sae releegious,' and he replied, 'Shairly it's the least Ah could dae — Ah wiz mairried til 'ur fur forty-fowr year.'

Of course, the women themselves play golf now, not always with male approval. Some Scots say: 'The best wey tae git yersel tae gie up gowff is tae learn yer missiz the ghemm.' And golf is not a great aid to romance. One lad tried to teach his 'finance' how to play, and one day she asked him on the course: 'Dae ye see ony improvement in me?'

'Oo ay,' he replied, 'ye've chynged yer hair-do.'

Women themselves usually have an extensive vocabulary of abuse, and if they are Lowland Scots speakers it can be very expressive and can be applied to other women, married and single!

'That yin wid gie kens-whit fur a man.' (That one would give goodness knows what for a man.)

'She's that shuttle-gabbit (crook-mouthed) that the loons lea her burdalane.' (All to herself.)

'Bella fancied a lad but he wiz owre coorse an' cyard-tonguit fur her tae tak hame.' (He swore like a tinker.)

67

'He turnt oot a richt slidderum (hypocrite), but she's taen up wi anither. A man huz just tae gie ae look at her an' she's fair cairrit.'

'She's a brent hizzie, that yin.' (A brazen-faced hussy.)

'She's sic a big, bamlan body, like the side o' a hoose, an' he's sic a wee smaik. Kin ye tell me hoo it is, the mair booksome they are, the mair like they are tae tak up wi some richt wee hoddle-madoak — an' shammle-shankit intil the bargain?'

'Oor Maggie'll nivver tak a man: she's owre *prignicketie*. It wid need tae be Aristoaly Parnassus fur that yin.'

'Noo, see oor Beenie? She's a chuffie wee bagrel (fatty), yet half the loons in the toon is trailin her like dugs efter a bickie.'

'Aweel, they wur only wan wee fluh hung aboot Tibby, an' he wiz aye owre tongue-tackit tae say whit he wiz efter.'

'Nae wunner the loon slichtit her at the feenish. She's sic a scowf (blusterer) owre nithing ava.'

But the loquaciousness of women in general is a masculine myth. Surely they are not all 'yatters, n'yatters, yatterers an' yiff-yaffs'. They cannot all be 'nebbie, nippety an' hillockit' (shrewish). It is a 'sclander' that leads to those tremulous poplar trees being known as 'auld wifes' tongues'. Why do fathers (and sometimes mothers) advise their sons: 'Nivver lat a lass git the owrance owre ye (the better of you).'

'Gabnash' (incessant talking), as 'the auld hech-how' (besetting sin) of the female, is undoubtedly what Women's Lib would call a masculine fantasy and stereotype.

'Weemen are aye moalygrantin (complaining).'

'Her moo's aye gaun like a mappie's.' (Her mouth is always going like a rabbit's.) Similarly, old women together are described as 'moopin like maukins' (making mouths like hares).

Another male fantasy is that women do not get off their mark in the morning. 'She bydes in bed till the neb's aff the day.'

Even that most gentlemanly of professions, the medical, has its moments of male chauvinism, though this is in decline with the increase in 'lassie doacters'. To a woman patient who wanted her tongue examined because she believed it was furred, one doctor testily replied: 'Na, na, lassie, ye dinnae git girss (grass) on a race-track.'

Another wifie, who was unduly 'booksome', complained she had lost her appetite, and he retorted: 'Goad help the quyne that finds it. Unless her man's a millionaire, they'll feenish up in the peers-hoose (poor-house).'

In some country parts the services of the doctor are not used so much as those of the 'druggist', as chemists are often called. One woman was asked by the 'druggist' if she had had any beneficial results from a patent medicine he had recommended to her, and she said: 'Dae me ony guid? For guidness sake! Ah read the prent aboot it on the wrapper, an' goat three mair ailments.'

Many of our traditional stories of the battle of the sexes are about encounters between women and ministers. One hospitable country wife was entertaining the minister and an elder, when the latter, after a hearty meal of tea and scones, catechized her with 'Whit dae ye think o the miracle o the loafs an' fishes?'

'Ah dinna richt ken fit tae mak o't, Mr Broon,' she said, 'but Ah'll tell ye this — gin yee an' the meenister had been there, there widna huv been aa that baskets o crumbs at the feenish.'

Another sterling character brought out her whisky bottle to give the minister 'a drap o the Auld Kirk'. He asked: 'Hoo auld is that whisky?'

'Ah dinna ken, meenister,' she said, 'but wi yee an' the elder ca'in by sae often, it'll nae git much aulder.'

Another wife was too discreet to pour her minister a glass of whisky, but, having a heart of gold, she slipped it in the glass of fresh milk she gane him, and, after he had quaffed it with satisfaction, asked him, 'Noo, food did ye like that?'

'Grand', he said, 'but, fitivver ye dee, nivver sell that coo!'

Another classic is of the 'gweedwife' who was pouring out the minister's tea when he commented in his stammering way: 'Yer t-teapot d-disna rin aafy weel.'

'Na,' said she, 'it's like yersel. It huz a gey peer deleevery.'

However, a country minister is alleged to have prayed aloud in church, 'Oh Loard, we thank Thee that Thou has creatit wumman tae make us comfortable.'

One religious wife was told by her angry husband, 'Ach, ye think a'body's gyann tae hell but ye an' the meenister.'

'Na ken,' she replied, 'Ah fyles hae ma doots aboot the meenister.'

A country minister refused to marry a young couple because the bridegroom turned up the worse for drink. 'Ah'll mairry ye whun he's sober,' said the preacher.

'But whun he's sober, he'll no come,' she said.

Scotswomen have been responsible for preserving many of our proverbs, sayings and phrases. Often the language is passed on by the 'auld wifes' rather than by the men, though in the cities it is perhaps the women who try to anglicize the speech of their boys and menfolk.

Some of the comments of the older generation of country women are rich. A useless young lassie ('a silly tawpie') is described as not being able to 'flype her huggers' (turn her stockings inside out).

How often we have heard of a neighbour wife who is putting on airs: 'She hudnae a sark til her back the day she goat merrit.'

'She speaks even on and nivver devaulds.' (Never ceases.)

'She gits in owre muckle o a curfuffle.' (She gets into too much of a state.)

'She jist gitters awa, daein jittry wark.'

'She's jist a trachle, aye in a harroch.'

Farther north, the wifies get in a 'boorach', a Gaelic word meaning a heap, and used in the Lowlands in the sense of a muddle.

'Eat up, noo! Wasters aye comes tae want.'

'That yin huz a tongue that wid clip cloots.' (She has a sharp tongue capable of cutting cloth.)

'Hoo are ye? Are ye brawly?'

'Ah'm aye huddin foarit.' (Always holding forward.)

'Ah'm geyan sober.' (I am not feeling very well!)

' "The mair hurry the less speed," quo' the wee tyler (tailor) til the lang threid.'

> 'Thur little wit intil the powe
> That lichts the caunle at the lowe.'
> (There's little sense in the head
> Of one who lights a candle at the fire.)

> 'Aye hae yer coggie oot whun it rains kail!'
> (Always have your bowl out when it rains broth.)

> 'Them that buys beef buys banes (bones):
> Them that buys land buys stanes (stones).'

> 'Heich hooses is aften tim in the tap storey.' (Haughty people are often lacking in sense — 'tim' means empty.)

> ' "Muckle cry an' little oo,"
> Quo' the Deil whun he clippit the soo.'
> ('A lot of noise and little wool,'
> Said the Devil when he sheared the sow.)

The Devil comes into many proverbs: ' "Hame's hame," as the Deil said whun he gaed til the Coort o Session.'

70

The donkey (cuddie) is another favourite in proverbial sayings: ' "That maks twa o's," as the coo said til the cuddie,' 'Ye'll git it whaur the coo calved the cuddie.' (You will *never* get it.)

'Dog don't eat dog,' I used to hear in Jamaica. In Scotland it is 'Coarbies (carrion crows) diznae pyke oot coarbies' een.'

Ah'm allooed tae titch it, but naebody else

There's fiddlin far the tinks are,
  Jock scarts wi rozet bow,
And owre the gress jig Jim and Jess
  And Jacquinet and Joe.

Listen fit the auld rogue
  Huz the nerve tae sing—
'The warl's tapsilteerie turned
  And ilka cove's a king.

'Geordie's King o England
  And Ah'm a king ma lane,
Wi a bonnie queen, a throne o green
  And a kingdom aa ma ain.

'Fa's the maister noo?
  Ilk Chamberlain and Cecil
And saft-soap lord and whisky duke
  Can crook his moo and fussle.'

One of the biggest tinker clans in Scotland is the Stewarts. But whether they are Stewarts or MacPhees, the 'cyards' consider themselves related to royalty, yet when a tink is on top of the world, he 'widna caa the King his kizzen (cousin)'. Now that we have a Queen, he perhaps might acknowledge kinship.

Because a James Stewart ascended to the English Throne, and the present Royal Family traces its ancestry back to that line, many Scots feel an affinity with the monarch. Hence the plethora of Royal names in many families. Most of my male relatives were Williams or Georges and there were Carolines and Victorias among the 'quynes' (just another form of 'queens', the status of all Scottish women).

Queen Victoria herself experienced the majesty of ordinary Scotswomen when she went to Holyrood Palace. She had never been keen on Holyrood, partly because it has always been surrounded by breweries and she was repelled by the smell of the mash. She stayed by preference at the residence of the Duke of Buccleuch, Dalkeith Palace.

However, on one occasion she and the Prince Consort (my namesake, need I say?) looked in at Holyrood informally and toured the historic chambers unannounced. One of the rooms she inspected was the bedroom of Mary Queen of Scots, from which Rizzio was dragged out to be murdered.

Everybody knows the room, where the bloodstains are still pointed out and occasionally, it is alleged, painted in.

Vicky put out a hand to examine the silk and embroidered hangings round her romantic and tragic ancestress's four-poster, and was immediately rebuked by an auld wife who had been watching her like a hawk since her arrival, and who happened to be a kind of caretaker.

'Ye're no allooed tae titch!' cried the wifie.

Queen Victoria protested: 'But I saw *you* touch it to show me.'

'Ay,' replied the woman, with a 'clip-cloots' tone in her voice, 'Ah'm allooed tae titch it, but naebody else!'

If it had been pointed out to her that she ought to have made an exception in the case of a Royal visitor, I am sure she would have claimed: 'Ah wiz nivver *tellt* onything like that.'

The reduction of Royalty to the status of the ordinary Scot is the theme of many old tales and of a popular barn-stormers' play, *Cramond Brig, or, The Guidman o' Ballengeich*. The play was based on the legend of Jock Howieson. This farmer near the River Almond, according to the story, rescued one of the Jameses (there is doubt whether it was James IV or James V) from highway robbers when the monarch was pursuing his hobby of riding around incognito. James, without disclosing his identity, invited the farmer to the palace, and told him he would know the King because everyone else would be bare-headed. When greeted at the palace by James, Jock is supposed to have said: 'Either you are the King, or me, for we baith hae keepit oor hats on.'

Descendants of Jock Howieson still have the honour of presenting basin and ewer to the monarch on a State visit to Scotland.

But the comical details of the legend go back beyond Cramond Brig. *The Taill of Rauf Coilzear, how he herberit King Charles* was published in St Andrews in 1572, and the only original copy appears to be the one in the National Library, Edinburgh. It is a translation or rather an adaptation, from a Norman tale. The King is Charlemagne but Rauf Coilzear (collier or charcoal burner) is very Scottish and so is the landscape, despite the fact that the setting is supposed to be France.

In this story Charlemagne, on his way to Paris, was cut off from his followers in a snowstorm:

> 'The wind blew oot of the east, stiffly and stour,
> The deep (snowdrift) durandlie (lastingly) drave in mony deep dell'.

Out on the wild 'muir' in the blinding storm, the King was lucky enough to meet a 'cant carl', the collier, and asked him to lead him to some 'herbery' (shelter).

Not knowing the King, and indeed rather wary of him, Rauf, when they reached the house, asked the great Charles to enter first, and, when the King demurred, pushed him into the house by the scruff of the neck, telling the monarch to do as he was told, and adding, 'Gif thou of courtasie couth, thou hes forget it clean' (If you ever learned manners, you have clean forgotten them.)

A repetition earned the King what we would now call 'a scud in the lug' —

> 'He let gird tae the King, withooten ony mair,
> And hit him under the ear with his richt hand.'

The King staggered 'half the breid of the hall', and did not know where he was until he hit the ground. Muhammad Ali could hardly have struck him harder.

Rauf gave him a stern lecture on his lack of respect for the 'heid o' the hoose', The story goes on to relate how Rauf at length discovers, at the palace, the King's identity, and how he becomes a knight and a Crusader. It is probable that the Jock Howieson story derived some of its humour from this and other legends.

Of more than one James it is related that he dressed up as a 'gaberlunyie' (beggar) man and went around playing pranks on ordinary Scots. Considering how many of the Stewart Kings came to a sticky and premature finish, and how many rebels there always were in Scotland, it must have been a risky ploy.

The Declaration of Arbroath, while hailing 'our lord Sir Robert (the Bruce)' as 'a second Maccabeus as it were or a Joshua', reminds even the national hero that, if he fails Scotland, another king will be appointed. In Latin it states: 'Were he to abandon the enterprise begun, choosing to subject us or our kingdom to the king of England or the English people, we would strive to thrust him out forthwith as our enemy and the subverter of right, and take for our king another who would suffice for our defence, for so long as an hundred remain alive we are minded never a whit to bow beneath the yoke of English dominion.'

Or, as Burns put it, 'A Man's a Man for A' That.'

Charles I was the last *native* King to be crowned in Scotland, and the last Scottish Coronation of all was that of Charles II at Scone on New Year's Day, 1651, when Cromwell was in Scotland — a typically Scottish act of defiance. At the Presbyterian service at Charles II's Coronation, the Reverend Robert Dowglas, Moderator of the Commission of the General Assembly, reminded Charles of the limitations of his monarchy: 'A king's power is a power limited by conditions.'

George IV, on his State visit in 1822, created merriment by his attempt to dress like a Scot, though one Highland laird described the King in his kilt as 'a verra pretty man'. Even more diverting to everyone at Holyrood was the apparition of a fat London alderman, Sir William Curtis, Baronet, in Highland garb, complete with *sgian dubh* (pronounced 'skeean doo', and alleged nowadays to mean a pigeon at Aviemore) stuck in his stocking. An Aberdonian is recorded as telling Sir William, 'Oo ay, the knife's aa richt, min, but far's yer speen?' (Where's your spoon?) That is the story told by Lockhart in his *Life of Sir Walter Scott*, but he throws a hint that Scott may have made up the bit about the Aberdonian.

Dinnae think, because Ah'm no sweerin, Ah'm no angry

The late Sir James Fergusson of Kilkerran (Jack House's partner in 'Round Britain Quiz' on the BBC, and brother of Sir Bernard, the 'monocled Chindit') records in *Lowland Lairds* the outburst of his ancestor, Sir Adam: 'Dinna think that because I'm no sweerin' I'm no angry.'

It is an illustration of the fact that, until recently, and *very* recently in the country parts and particularly in the North East, the upper and middle classes could express themselves fluently in the vernacular.

Braid Scots is the great leveller, and, if farm workers and other employees find it effective in letting off steam at their employers, the latter have been known to make just as effective use of it in retaliation.

It is only in the past couple of generations that it has tended to peter out among the educated Scots, and even there it is always demonstrating that it is capable of a comeback. Sir Walter Scott normally spoke broadly, as when he saw the steeple of Tron Kirk go up in flames, in the Edinburgh High Street fires, and exclaimed: 'Hech sirs, mony a weary sermon hae I heard aneath that steeple!'

Robert Louis Stevenson spoke Scots, and wrote it without difficulty, as did many another Edinburgh advocate. David Hume, the philosopher who is noted for his meticulous avoidance of 'Scotticisms' in his writing, is recorded by contemporaries as being 'broader in speech' than Robert Burns, who liked to show, both in conversation and in his elaborate letters, that he was 'nae sheep-shank bane' when it came to 'knappin Suthron.'

Stevenson, in one letter, wrote 'Kinnigam' for 'Cunningham' (his old nurse's name). He knew he was recognized in Edinburgh as 'the lang lean chiel in the velvet jaicket'. If he ever forgot, he was reminded by the wee 'keelies' in George Street shouting after him:

> 'Half a laddie,
> Half a lassie,
> Half a yellie-yite (yellowhammer)!'

In the Royal Hotel in Bathgate, Stevenson noticed that the maid was gazing intently out of the window. He asked her: 'What are you looking for?' and she replied: 'Ah'm lookin fur ma lad.'

'Is *that* him?' Stevenson enquired, pointing to someone passing

'Keep it an' git yer hair cut!'

outside, and received the answer: 'Weel, Ah've been lookin fur him aw ma life, an' Ah've nivver seen him yet.'

Another Edinburgh character, Professor John Stewart Blackie, experienced the ready retorts of the local 'keelies' when he was walking in Princes Street. Blackie wore his hair to his shoulders and went around in a broad-brimmed hat and a plaid, carrying a shepherd's crook. At that time (as within living memory) there was a street drinking fountain on an island between the Caledonian Hotel and the West End fashion shops. Approaching the fountain, Blackie noticed a small boy, with a dirty face, hanging about there, probably waiting to help some railway passenger with luggage and make 'a wing or a bob'.

Blackie, noticing the grubbiness of the street-arab, said: 'I'll give you sixpence if you wash your face at that fountain!'

The boy replied: 'Keep it an' git yer hair cut!'

It was Blackie who put up a notice in the Old Quadrangle of the University that he would 'meet his classes' at a certain time. The inevitable smart-Alec student scored out the *c* and made it read: 'Professor Blackie will meet his *lasses*...' Blackie quickly detected the act of sabotage, and removed the *l*, to announce that he would 'meet his *asses*'.

As evidence that fluency in Scots did not die out with the middle-class generation of the Stevensons and Blackies, one of the most prolific writers in Scots in my own university days was a professor of economics, Sir Alexander Gray, who translated the poems of Heine, and many German and Scandinavian lyrics, into our tongue.

Once, when I was editor of the *Edinburgh Evening Dispatch*, I sent a reporter to interview Sir Alexander on some topical monetary point, something to do with the state of the pound sterling, and the reporter came back empty-handed. A little later I met Sir Alec by chance in a cloakroom, and told him I was disappointed that he had not given my representative an interview. His reply was:

'Ah dinna gie ma views on current affairs. On tap o that — Ah'm nae a verra guid economist.' This was in contrast to the professor's oratorical style, which was very 'Standard English'.

The best area for repartee in the vernacular between the classes is the North-East, where everybody, linguistically, tends to be on an equal footing. Railway carriages were often the setting.

Although, Scots, especially on the East Coast (including Edinburgh), are reserved in their approach to strangers, they hate nothing more than to get their 'neb in a sling' when they *do* break the silence.

One traveller asked the man sitting opposite him: 'Are ye fur Kitty-brewster, than?'

'No.'

A little later: 'Are ye fur Aiberdeen?'

'No.'

The questions ceased. Soon the train pulled up at a station and the 'spierer' got out. He banged the compartment door shut after him, and snapped through the open window: 'Dae ye think Ah care a damn *far* (where) ye're gyann?'

In another carriage, a Banffie farmer found himself opposite a professor of agriculture. They got on to farming topics, and the landsman commented: 'Ye'll nae ken muckle aboot the fermin, like?'

'Excuse me!' said the affronted scholar, 'I happen to be a professor of *agriculture*.'

'Aweel, ye'll nae ken muckle aboot the fermin.'

'I think I could hold my own with you any day. I'll give a pound for every question on farming you care to ask me and which I can't answer, if you will agree to give me a pound for any question I ask *you* and *you* can't answer.'

'Ah, but byde a bit!' said the canny cultivator. 'Ye're an educatit chiel, an' Ah'm jist a fermer. Ah'll gie ye fifty pence for onything ye spier at me that Ah canna answer, an' ye'll gie me a pound gin Ah stump ye. Is that nae fair, conseederin ye hae the owrance o me that nivver wiz at neen o yer grammer squeels or dirt coalleges?'

'Very well, then. I agree.'

So they went at it, 'spier fur spier', and neither of them got the 'owrance' of the other, until, near the farmer's station, he suddenly posed the professor with: 'Fit is't, noo? It huz sax legs, it's nae a bird, it's nae an inseck, an' it fussles an' it flees.'

'I don't know the answer to that one,' confessed the professor, and immediately handed over a pound. The train stopped and the farmer got out, pocketing the spoil.

'Ah — But wait a minute!' said the professor, jumping to the window and talking to the man on the platform. 'You haven't told me the *answer*.'

'Na,' said the farmer, '*Ah* dinna ken, *neither*. There's yer fifty pence!'

Scottish judges at one time were fluent in Scots, and Lord Braxfield in particular is famous for his Court declarations in the vernacular, such as 'Ye're a clever chiel but ye'll be nane the waur o a hangin.'

A Lord Justice-Clerk (the second highest member of the Scottish judiciary) got the worst of an encounter in the common tongue. He was walking through a turnip-field in an Edinburgh suburb, when the market gardener hailed him with 'Heh, you! Come oot amun thae neeps!'

By way of assuring the objector that he was a responsible citizen, the judge told him: 'I'm the Lord Justice-Clerk.'

'Ah dinnae gie a damn *whaes* clerk ye are!' roared the other. 'Come oot amun thae neeps!'

Lord Polkemmet, a Scottish judge, is recorded by Dean Ramsay as saying to a guest, who was surprised at all the dishes being of veal: 'Oo ay, it's cauf: when we kill a beast we just eat it up ae side and doon the tither.'

Lord Cockburn reports the same of Miss Menie Trotter of Mortonhall, who lived in the original Blackford House in Edinburgh. Not long before her death, she invited Sir Thomas Dick Lauder, her neighbour of Grange, to dine with her on what was left of an ox, which she had the custom of eating from nose to tail. Urging him to come to Sunday dinner, the old maid added: 'For eh, Sir Tammas, we're terrible near the tail noo!'

It was about the same time that, on being asked how she was, she replied: 'Verra weel, quite weel; but eh, Ah had a dismal dream last nicht, a fearfu dream.'

'Oh, Ah'm sorry tae hear that. What was it?'

'Oo, whit d'ye think? Of aw places in the world, Ah dreamt Ah wiz in Heeven! An' whit d'ye think Ah saw there? Deil haet but thoosands upon thoosands, and ten thoosands upon ten thoosands, o' stark nakit wains! That wid be a dreidfu thing — for ye kin Ah neer could byde bairns aw ma days.'

That was our middle-class — or, as they say in the Borders, 'oor hauf-nabs' or 'hauf-nabberie', before the practice of sending their children to 'public schools' ironed out their tongues.

Another of the tales of Lord Braxfield is of his answer to a butler who gave his notice because the judge's wife was always scolding him. Said his lordship: 'Man, ye've little tae complain o. Ye may be thankfu ye're no mairrit tae her.'

Bizzin aboot the dirt like a shairny flee

Part of the appeal of dialect is its touch of the primitive. Scots words take us back to somewhat less sophisticated conditions. By a perverse streak in human nature we are sometimes nostalgic about the so-called 'guid auld days', which were in many ways not so good as all that.

Adam must have felt that way about the Garden of Eden from which he had been expelled, forgetting that, back there, he was bothered with snakes and uncomfortable prohibitions. Many Scots look back to a childhood in which sanitation, in particular, had not reached its present stage of development.

Sir Walter Scott, born in the Old Town of Edinburgh, with its street dung-heaps, its lack of household water and its slaughter-men throwing their refuse into the North Loch within smelling distance of the high tenements, looked back with such nostalgia from his Georgian residence in the New Town. You can detect his affection for the scruffy past in his *Heart of Midlothian* and other Waverley Novels. *Nostalgie de la boue*, the French call it — a longing to get back and roll in the mud.

When King James VI ascended the English Throne in 1603 he was glad to get away from his native city, and when he was due back on a State visit, there was a great fuss about clearing the 'middens' from what is now called the Royal Mile — then the main street of the Capital. Edinburghers were still huddled on the slope between the Castle and the Palace, in the oldest 'skyscrapers' in the world, with all classes in the one building or 'land', and water carried to the aristocrats' flats by porters.

When the New Town was built, there were still many who preferred the Old, probably on the Scottish argument, 'The clartier the cosier.'

I suppose it is partly as a consequence of the grim realism of those days that much of our family humour even now is of the 'coorse' variety. Of many a Scot it is said that he is 'aye bizzin aboot the dirt like a shairny flee (always buzzing around the refuse like a coprophagous fly)', or 'He's aye *there*, or *thereaboot*'.

'Dirt' itself is one of the commonest words to describe gossip. In the North they ask: 'Fit's the dirt?' for 'What's the latest?' and many a woman is described as having 'Lugs like a mechanical sheel (shovel) fur pickin up the dirt.'

It is not so long, after all, since the 'midden' and the outside dry

80

closet were features of everyday life in country towns and villages. Even now, in Glasgow, you hear dust-carts called 'midden-cairts'.

There is the typical Glasgow joke about the 'scaffies' (scavengers') picnic at 'Rossie' where 'Joack wiz that unyaized wi the fresh err that he faintit, an' they hud tae hud him owre a midden tae revive him.'

Billy Connolly's 'sterrheid' and 'cluggie' (loo) humour is in tradition.

Edinburgh was famous for its cry of 'Gardyloo!' (from pseudo-French *'Gare de l'eau'* — Watch out for the water!) when, as Robert Fergusson put it, the lassies 'poured Edina's roses' from the tenement windows. It is said that there are still such conditions in some parts of the city, but nowadays they don't give the polite warning cry.

There is a wealth of synonyms for the closet, which, until too recently, was shared among several families in slum tenements — it is variously called the 'shunkie', 'duffie', 'oaffie' (probably from 'office'). More politely it is 'the Hoose o Parlyment'.

Similarly, the convenient household utensil has a wealth of names from 'jordan' to 'pattie' and the most widely used of all — 'chantie'.

A country lassie taken into Edinburgh Royal Infirmary saw a hospital bed-pan for the first time in her life, as it was being taken away by a nurse from a nearby bed.

'Heh!' she cried, laughing, to the sister, 'that fat wife huznae half flettened yer chantie.'

For the facts of life generally, the Scottish dialects are well-equipped. The local philanderer or 'pairish bull' is known as a 'dyke-lowper', meaning he jumps over various garden walls in his amorous pursuits.

'Baggit', in the case of a man, may mean merely corpulent, but when applied to a young woman it means big with child.

'He's been fleein his draigon' (flying his kite), the 'country clypes' say of a man they suspect of being responsible for an illicit 'bairnin'.

A man who has run out on his girl friend is said to have 'jeckit' (abandoned) her, but the word is applied also to a girl jilting a man. Nowadays a loon is just as likely to be 'begunkit, begowkit an' begoogled' as a quyne. This is what 'Weemen's Leeb' is all about.

Girls are well supplied with words to downgrade the gallants, or raw 'callants' — 'He's jist a muckle gaivie', 'Ah nivver wiz oot wi sic a gammarackus', 'If he's no a gamphrel, he's a gommeril an' a gilliegawkus.' If Scotland had a Roget's *Thesaurus* it would supply also *gonial, gowk, gumph, rammlegawkus, rammlekyte, stump, sumph* and *stymalt* for 'a daft eejit'. Even 'a silly tawpie' can get her own back by calling her boy-friend 'a tumshy-heid' (turnip-head).

A light-headed person, male or female, may be described as 'corkie-heidit' or 'corkie-noddled'. But it is applied particularly to girls, who may also be 'skeeriemalinkies' and 'fliskmahoys', as well as being, in the sense of chatterers, 'gashpots', 'hashmagandies' and 'claivers'. It is some compensation to be known otherwise as 'a dentie quyne' or a 'weel-faurd' or 'tidy kimmer'. A conceited girl is a 'croose lass'.

'Luckie' used to be the epithet applied to an older woman, and in Edinburgh it was the title usually of some woman who kept an ale-house — 'luckie Middlemiss', 'Luckie Dundas' and so on. But in Perthshire a woman who is a bit of a character may be called 'a gey luckie'. 'Gey' (usually meaning rather) is often applied in this way to both sexes — 'A gey lad, thoan!'

Derogatory epithets applied to women are 'jauds', 'cutties', 'limmers' and 'bizzims'; very wild lassies are 'hempies' and useless ones are 'tim pease-coads' (empty pea-pods).

As to the physical attractions of the lassies, Scots is inclined to be specific. Perhaps she has a 'jimp pair o kits', a neat pair of ankles, which in the North becomes a 'gweed pair o queets' and in Caithness a 'geed pair o keets'. They like a lassie or a quyne to be 'swack' (well set-up) or, as they say in some places, 'swank' and, in others, just 'clivver'. Even when dressed in a 'scodgie brat' (a coarse working apron), she can be a 'smasher', though other women will say, 'She's nae burnin beauty', or 'She's nae *barnyaird* beauty'.

If the poor lass is employed in an 'assiepan' (drudgery) capacity, she may have difficulty in avoiding being an 'assiepet' or just a dirty 'clatch', with a 'brukit' (grubby) face, her 'claes' (clothes) 'aw rampoozled' (all disarranged), and her hair 'in a hugger', or 'aw huggerie-muggerie'.

But just you wait till she 'straichens' her hair and does up her 'brees' (eyebrows) and puts that shadow stuff on her 'eewinkers' (eyelids)! She will be 'tittiebillie (a match) wi the best o them'.

'Aince she geets giein her neck a dicht' (has a chance to wash her neck) and cleans herself 'abin the dirliebanes' (above the elbows), instead of just giving herself 'a coo's lick' or 'a lick an' a proamise', and gets 'horkin oot her braws' (raking out her best dresses), you will see the 'wee banyel' or 'walliedrag' 'fair transmugrifeed' intil 'a tidy kimmer' and it will be a question of 'Wha's gittin her?' (Who is the lucky man?)

Of course there will still be those who will say: 'The loon that fancies *her's* nae richt allister' (not of sound mind).

In the countryside we are near to nature, and so words tend to be precise and unpretentious. A Perthshire farmer was a great believer in 'naitral' (natural) fertilizer, and was proud of his long-standing arrangement with the neighbouring pony-trekking establishment. So, when his daughter brought her boy-friend to have a tour of the farm, the father took it upon himself to accompany them, and indeed act as a very informative guide.

His word for the fertilizer was 'mainer', and he kept pointing out where it had been applied and the benefits accruing therefrom. Now the boy was not even a 'dirt student' or remotely connected with the land, and the girl thought she detected some curling of the nostrils in the course of the conducted tour.

When she got home she complained to her mother: 'Ma, Ah wish ye wid get Dad tae stoap speaking aboot mainer.'

'Lassie,' said her mother, 'whit you dinnae appreciate is the years it's taen me tae git him tae *use* that word!'

A much older farmer surprised a friend with his answer to 'Fit like?'

'Min, Ah'm nae bad, but Ah'm haein an aafa bother wi sex.'

'Michty me, min, fit's an aal man like you deein botherin aboot sex?'

'That's jist it,' said the veteran. 'Ah've that fowr acres o tatties, an' Ah canna get *secks* (sacks) fur love or money.'

Whit wid Ah want wi a spin-dryer?

Braid Scots may be fighting a rearguard action in the battle of keeping up with the Joneses — or the 'Joansins'. A wifie the other day was at one of those 'cleckins o auld hens' where the conversation soon drifts round to 'Scots wha hae — and Scots wha hinnae'.

She was asked by a superior 'neebor wife': 'Hev you not got a spin-dryer?'

'Michty me!' she replied. 'Whit wid Ah want wi a spin-dryer? Ah jist dry ma spins (spoons) oan the dishtool (kitchen-cloth).'

That is a south-of-Firth-and-Clyde joke, for over in Fife they do not say 'spin' for 'spoon'. They say 'Spain'. And by the time you get to Keith they are saying 'speen'. So it is not much of a joke to Banffie,

Morayshire or Aberdonian ears.

In Perthshire they say 'spune' and in Shetland 'spön' — almost the same sound. It should rhyme with the German *schön*; the vowel is like French, *eu* in *un peu*, or the *oeu* in *hors d'oeuvres*.

Even the 'kye' (cows) understand different sounds in different parts of Scotland. In Melrose and Hawick it may be all right to say 'Troo leddy!' to get the cow to come in for milking. But an Aberdeen, or even an Edinburgh, 'coo' would ignore you unless you said 'Trooy', and in Shetland the 'leddy' would be very hoity-toity unless you said 'trow'. I suppose the important thing is to remember to call the cow a lady.

All sorts of funny things happen to words in odd corners of the realm. I have just heard of an old lady, a friend of a friend, who had heard of a bank clerk up to some hanky-pany, and said: 'Ah dinnae ken hoo he managed tae *bamboozle* aw that money.'

In parts of the Borders 'a lump sum' becomes a 'slump', which must be confusing to local economists.

All over Scotland I have heard the ferrule of a walking-stick or umbrella called a 'virl'. Some old ladies make their state of 'nerves' sound more tense by calling it 'nervishness': 'Thae new neebors huz me that nervish wi their grammyphone.'

They learn new words from their grandchildren, but prefer their own way of saying them. One spoke of her grandson 'soomin unner the watter wi his *snorple* oan.'

Medical terms are introduced with such rapidity nowadays that even doctors must find it hard to keep abreast of them. So can we blame the wifie who says: 'Noo they're tryin tae tell me ma man is sufferin fae a *clestril* through drinkin owre much milk. Ah'm shair *that* yin nivver drank enough milk tae gie him a clestril.'

Modern gadgets get their own Scots names, resurrected from the past and fitted to the present. The spin-dryer becomes a 'birler' and the supermarket trolley becomes a 'hurlie', from the 'hurlbarra' (wheelbarrow) of old. The 'tellie' and the 'trannie' have found their natural place in the vernacular, just as the 'airyplane' did long ago.

A relatively new word, such as 'fluorescent', soon gets the treatment, and becomes 'flooery-scentit', whether it is applied to office lighting or to a lollypop man's 'weskit'.

It is somehow easier to say 'essiclater' than 'escalator' and, in industrial disputes, to threaten that the action will 'essiclate' as soon as 'bad management' sets in.

I sat in a bus recently and heard an old man tell a girl across the 'aizly' that he had 'whit they caw a runnin *ulster*', and almost the same day I met someone who had a 'hae-tae-us' hernia.

The same people have no difficulty in getting those awkward old Scots words right, such as 'fizzionless' for lacking pith, and 'dauchelt' for tired out: 'Ah feenished up fair dauchelt wi aw the trauchle!'

They can diagnose old familiar ailments such as the 'molligrumphs': 'Ah cannae be daein wi her whun she taks thae molligrumphs.' And they can say 'waukrife' (wakeful), 'meatrife' (well off for meat) and 'teethrife' (toothsome) without hesitation: 'Thoan wiz aye a meatrife hoose. Ah've nivver haen a mair teethrife steak.'

They have 'lang-nebbit words' of their own. 'He's jist a furritsome (officious) wee smaik.' 'Ye cannae whack oor meenister fur a driech, *teedisome* sermon.' And they can add syllables to 'oarner', everyday words. For instance, 'safety' is often pronounced 'safey-tae', even when it is just used for a 'safey-tae peen'.

And do not 'craw doon yer neb' at the grammar of Scots speakers. Almost all the strange ways they have of saying things are to be found in 'Shakespeare's pure well of English undefiled'. My curiosity on this point was aroused to the extent that I read the complete works of the Bard and discovered he was almost certainly 'wanny *uz*' (one of us) or else took lessons from James VI and I.

Shakespeare even wrote 'ken' for 'know'. In *Troilus and Cressida* he has Ulysses say: 'Tis he, I ken the manner of his gait.' Rabbie Burns would not have put it differently.

In *A Midsummer Night's Dream*, Bottom asks the fairy Mustard-seed to give him his 'neif' — or 'nieve' as we say in Edinburgh. We think of 'mickle' or 'muckle' as the Scots for 'much', and we have placenames such as Muckle Flugga. But Shakespeare uses the same word in *Henry VI, Part I*: 'Tomorrow I shall die with mickle age.'

He even writes 'fell' for 'fallen' (as in 'Get fell in, yous!') 'He would have dropp'd his knife and fell asleep' (*Titus Andronicus*). '...have with one winter's brush *Fell* from their boughs' (*Timon of Athens* — I wonder if that had anything to do with 'Jenny Athens'?)

Here are some similar sentences, which schoolboys would have been 'beltit', or 'meltit', for, in my day, but Shakespeare got away with: 'That I would have *spoke of.*' (*Timon of Athens*). 'Your words have *took* such pains.' (*Timon* again). 'He is so *shaked.*' (Henry V). 'Which was *broke* off.' (*Measure for Measure*). 'And thereupon these errors are *arose.*' (*Comedy of Errors*). 'Ay, but I shall think that it is *spoke* in hate.' (*Two Gentlemen of Verona*). 'O, no, he lives but is *took* prisoner... Most of the rest slaughtered and *took* likewise.' (*Henry VI*

85

...or else (Shakespeare) took lessons from James VI and I

Part I).

Now, in Glasgow and Edinburgh we hear orators saying 'furty' (for to), as in 'it is high time *furty* get weavin on social improvements...' And here is 'yer Wullie Shakespeare': 'Here lacks but your mother *for to* say Amen... To send down justice *for to* wreak our wrongs' (*Titus Andronicus*). '... You may as well Forbid the sea *for to* obey the moon.' (*A Winter's Tale*).

> 'Neighbours and friends, though bride and bridegroom wont
> *For to* supply the places at the table...' (*Taming of the Shrew*).

> '... let your highness
> Lay a more noble thought upon mine honour
> Than *for to* think that I would sink it here.' (*All's Well.*)

Like a good Scotsman he used 'broke' for 'broken', 'learn' for 'teach', 'catch'd' for 'caught' and 'remember' for 'remind'. Who knows but what, instead of being Bacon in disguise, he was really 'Jamie the Saxt' having fun with the Suthrons, with help from his Border jester, 'Erchie Ermstrang'.

He even used such Scottish words as 'boggle' (to hesitate), 'brock' (a badger), 'check' (to give a telling-off), 'claw' (to scratch or flatter), 'feared' (frightened), 'file' (to dirty), 'prig' (a thief, a favourite word with Lothian and Border policemen), 'punk' (a lewd person, now back in full swing as 'punk rock'), and 'younker' (youngster). About thirteen of his thirty-seven plays were written after Jamie went to London, but the Scottish King was inviting English 'comedians' to Edinburgh long before that, and how can we be certain that he did not lend them a hand with their scripts?

As for those new scientific words, an Edinburgh schoolboy swears 'nuclear fission' originally meant 'fishin' for 'bairdies, doacters an' baggy minnens' in his favourite 'neuk' in Puddocky on the Water of Leith. And though he had never heard of silicon chips, he knows all about 'haddock an' chips'.

A professor of micro-electronics had a rush to catch the seaside train at Waverley, and just threw himself into a corner seat. As the train scurried out he noticed a schoolgirl sitting in the opposite corner giving him a baleful stare. He looked down, to find he was sitting on a newspaper, and, presuming it was hers, pulled it out from under him and handed it to her. She took it with a tear starting in her eye, so he asked: 'Is that not what you wanted?'

She blurted out: 'Naw, it's the *haddock an' chips* that wiz *in* it.'

That cows the cuddie an' the cuddie cows aw

Mark Twain, in his introduction to *Huckleberry Finn*, worries in case his readers think his characters are 'trying to speak alike and not succeeding', and pleads that he is writing in a variety of dialects. There is a similar explanation for what may look like inconsistencies in spelling in this book.

There is, in fact, almost a different dialect for each of the five million inhabitants of Scotland. Some of the individual pronunciations are recorded here:

AIRNMAIL	Rusty stains on clothes.
ALCOVE	Old man in Keith.
ALLACREESH	Licorice, also known as 'sugarellie', 'sugar-allie'.
ALLEY	A boy's 'bool' or marble, from 'alley-baster'.
AWANTIN	Missing: 'He's goat three fing-urs awantin.'
AWGAIT	Everywhere: 'She's been sallyvoogan awgait.'
AWTHING	Everything. 'Jenny' or 'Joahnny Awthing', a small shopkeeper who sells 'awthing fae a needle til an anchor'.
BAMPOT	Dead loss; also 'bamstick'.
BAR-L	Barlinnie.
BELDIE	Bald: 'Dinnae git beldie-heidit owre it (Keep your hair on)!'
BIRKIE	Smart youth.
BLACKAVEEZED	Dark-featured, but not 'coloured'.
BLATE	Backward, shy: 'Here, you're no blate!'
BOIL	Snob-word for 'bile': 'Snuffty gie ye the boil.'
BOOLER	Player of bowls. A 'bowler' is a round hat.
BOOZER'S LABOURER	Lounge waiter.
BOWDIE	Bow-legged: 'That yin's awfy bowdie-leggit.'
BUCKIE	Sea-shell; refractory child: 'Ah'll cloor ye, ye young buckie!'
BUNCE	'Halfers': 'Ah'll bunce ye!' 'We'll gang buncers.'

CAUNLE DOWP	Candle end.
CHACKERS	Teeth: 'Pit that in yer chackers an' stoap yer mumpin!'
CLAW	Scratch: 'Awa'n' claw!' (Away and don't bother me!)
CLEVERALITY	Smart Alec: 'That's eneuch o you, Cleverality!'
COANTERMASHUS	Perverse.
COWSTICK	Sarcastic: 'Ye neednae be sae doggont cowstick.'
CUDDIE	Donkey: 'That cows (beats) the cuddie an' the cuddie cows aw (beats all).'
CUDDIE WECHTS	A rough boys' game also known as 'Gie wey!'
CULLIEBUCKIE	Pickaback; also, 'colliebackie', 'carryback', 'piggyback'.
CUNYIE NEUK	Cosy corner, also a cushy job.
DAD	Father; also a lump: 'Fancy a dad o' cheese, Dad?'
DAW	Jackdaw; also, 'kay'. 'Ye cannae flee wi the daws an' roost wi the craws.'
DELEERIT	Mad, as if from DTs.
DEW	A personal question: 'Dew fancy yersel, like?'
DICHT	A careless wash: 'Ah jist gied ma face a dicht.'
DOWP	Posterior; sit: 'The day's dowpin doon.'
DOWPS	Cigarette ends; also, 'dowts'.
DROOND	Drown: 'Ah wiz oot in that shoor (shower) an' goat fair droondit.'
DROOTH	Drought, thirst, heavy drinker.
DUMB SWEER	Putting thumb to nose.
ELECTRIT	Political orator's word for voters.
EQUAL-ACQUAL	Fair shares
EVEN OAN	Continually: 'It dang (pelted with rain) even oan.'
EVERLESTIN	A long time: 'She yammert oan fur a guid everlestin.'
FAN	Found; also 'when', in Northern speech.

FASH	Worry: 'Dinna fash yersel!'
FAW TAE	Fall to; start eating!
FERNIETICKLE	Freckle: 'A richt fernietickelt reed-heid.'
FISTICAT	A what-d'ye-call-it, thingummyjig.
FIT THE FLEER	Foot the floor, dance (North).
FIT-WASHIN	Foot-washing, an Orkney bridal ritual.
FRUESOME	Frowzy: 'We aye gied her (called her) Fruesome Freedie.'
FULLIE	A full-sized football.
FYKE	A poor eater.
GALLUSES	Gents' braces: 'Ah think he's goat paralysis o the galluses.'
GIBBIE	A tom-cat; Gibson.
GIRNIEGOWGUBBIE	A complaining child.
GERMANIC	Neighbourly concern: 'Germanic come yet tae read the meter?'
GLADIOLI	Gratitude: 'Ye should be gladioli done fur ye.'
GOATH	Fife word for pub (Gothenburg).
GOWPIN	Double fistful: 'That guy huz gowpins o gowd' (He's rich).
GRANNY	'Ah wish ma granny saw ye' (cat-call in song, 'Johnny Raw').
GRIEVIOUS	Terrible: 'Ye gien us aw a *grievious* affront wi yer *mischievious* kerry-oan.'
HAAF	Sea (Shetland); 'da far haaf', or 'da blue joob', the deep.
HAAFMEN	Sea fishers.
HACKUMPLACKUM	A fair day's pay for a fair day's work: 'Hack (hire) him; plack (pay) him.'
HANLA-WHILE	A wee whilie: 'Kin ye no byde still a hanla-while?'
HEY-MA-NANNIE	At great speed: 'He beetled aff like hey-ma-nannie.'
HUNKER	Haunch, squat miner-style, 'hunkert doon'.
HUNKERSLIDIN	Reneging.
IDDER	Other (Shetland).
ILL-FAURED	Ugly.

IMPETENCE	Cheek: 'Ye've as muckle impetence as the miller's horse.'
INGAIT	Entrance: 'Thoan braw brig at the ingait o Kelsay.'
INGAN JOAHNNIE	A Breton onion-seller.
JAMAICA	A nosey-parkerism: 'Jamaica pile oan ra moonlightin?'
JAUP	Splash: 'Ye've went an' stepped in ra dub an' *Ah* goat awra jaups.'
JEMIMA	Hopeful approach in a pub or 'howff': 'Jemima face?'
JENNYWURRY	January: 'Jennywurry wi yer Income-tax?'
JINGLEJYNTIT	Rickety, often applied to furniture.
JOAHNNY	Sisterly concern: 'Joahnny luck at the bingo?'
KAIL	Colewort, broth, a telling-off: 'Ye'll git yer kail through the reek whun the wife sees ye.'
KEEKER	Black eye.
KEN	Know: 'Ye ken yer ain ken best.'
KENNLE	Kindle: 'Ah couldnae even kennle a spark in um.'
KENSPECKLE	Well-known, prominent, conspicuous.
KEPPERS	'Catchers', children's game.
KERRIOUS	Curious.
KERMUD	Thick as thieves: 'They're owre kermud, that twa.'
KINNAWEYS	In a way, to some extent.
KIP	Play truant: also 'plunk' and 'plug' (the 'skill', 'scule' or 'squeel').
KISSEN	Cast: 'The pair o them's kissen oot.'
KYTE	Big belly: 'He hud sic a kyte awbody kent him as "Kytie".'
LAPPER	Curdle: 'Her face wid lapper aw the toon's milk.'
LASHGELAVVIE	Extravagantly: 'Awbody's livin owre lashgelavvie noo.'
LASHINS	Plenty: 'Rerr digs, an' lashins o meat.'
LESKIT	Elastic: 'Ah could dae wi yer leskit fur ma guttieputt (catapult).'

91

LICENIN	Licencing, as pronounced on a political platform.
LICHTLIFEE	Disparage: 'It's nae kerrit story, sae ye neednae lichtlifee it.'
LINTIE	Linnet: 'Aff she gaed singan like a lintie.'
LIPPEN	Trust: 'Dinna lippen yer back til a fail (turf) dyke!'
MANNIE	Little man; mustn't: 'Weel, ma mannie, Ah mannie keep ye.'
MANT	Stammer: 'Ah couldnae mak oot whit he wiz mantin at.'
MASK	Brew, infuse: 'Gie the tea time tae mask.'
MAUCHIE	Muggy; maggoty.
MAUN	Must: 'Them that will tae Cupar maun tae Cupar.'
MOARNIN	First drink of the day: 'A fine moarnin, missiz!' 'Ay, but hauf o't's fur anurra wumman.'
MOOTHIE	Mouth-organ, harmonica.
MOOTHFY	Mouthful: 'You an' yer "Ah'll jist hae a moothfy"! Ye'll hae a pint the same as the rest.'
NAEGAIT	Nowhere, 'no way': 'It diznae geet ye naegait.'
NIPPETY	Sharply critical: 'She kin be gey nippety, whiles.'
NUCKLE-LATE	Inoculate: 'Ah'll no tak nae flu: Ah've been nucklelatit agane it.'
NORATION	Clamour: 'Ah cannae be daein wi a busload o weemen wi aw that noration.'
OARNER	Ordinary: 'Kin ye no eat purritch like oarner folk?'
OCH AY THE NOO	English idea of Scottish speech: 'Did ye hear about the Scotchman that was made chief of a Red Indian tribe? They called him "Hawk Eye the Noo".'
ONYGAIT	Anywhere: 'Gin ye fin it onygait, ye're a wonder.'

OO	Lothian and Borders, we; also, wool. 'Aw ae oo' (All one wool).
OOR YINS	Our family (South); farther north it becomes 'oor anes' or 'oor eens'.
OOTDICHTINS	Left-overs; 'Ootdichtins fae the rich man's table.'
PEENIE	Pinafore.
PEENIE ROSES	Peonies.
PLATFITTIT	Flatfooted: 'Dinnae walk sae platfittit, ye big juck!'
PLUNKER	Large marble in game of 'bools'.
PUGGIE	Monkey: 'Gin ye pey puggie-nits (peanuts), ye'll geet puggies warkin fur ye.'
PYOKE	Bag in North; elsewhere, 'poke'. 'Ah'm nae buyin nae pig in a pyoke.'
QUEEN	A girl; 'quyne' farther north. A very old usage as any university student who has endured the rigours of Anglo-Saxon will tell you; 'cwen' in Old English meant simply 'woman', not a female monarch.
QUYNIE	A little girl.
RANNIGAL	Rascal; renegade.
RIGG	Ridge: 'Happin aboot like craws on a rigg.'
RUMMLEGUMPTION	Commonsense.
RUMMLESHACKIN	Loose-jointed: 'A muckle, rummleshackin carl.'
SCAFFIE-BUCKET	Dustbin.
SHOO	Sew.
SKELF	Splinter of wood, also 'spale': 'Dinnae scart yer heid or ye'll git skelfs in yer fing-urs!'
SKLEFF	Flat, even: 'Oo're skleff noo' (We're quits); 'Ah've a skleff wame (I've a flat tummy — I'm hungry).'
SLEPPINN	Overslept: 'Please, miss, Ah sleppinn.' Alternative excuse: 'Ah wiz keepin the lodger's bed warm.'
SMAIK	A mean little fellow: 'Ye dirty wee smaik!'

SOMEGAIT	Somewhere: 'Ah hope ye'll come acroass it somegait.'
SONSIE	Plump: 'Fair fa' your honest, sonsie face'. (Burns)
SOOK	Teacher's pet: 'Ye're a sook, an' a clype forbye.'
STEELT	Stolen: 'Some'dy's went and steelt the collection.'
STREW	It's a fact.
SWAY	It's a goner: 'Sway fur ile!' 'Him? Sway wirra ferries.'
SWEAT	It's a rainy day.
TATTIE-BASHER	Potato-masher.
THREEP	Argue: 'Dinnae you threep doon *ma* throat!' 'Keep yer threep!' (Keep your opinions to yourself!)
TIG	The game of 'tag', 'tip-and-run'. 'Tig you're het, an' *Ah'm* no playin.'
TIMMER	Wooden: 'A timmer weskit' (a coffin); 'Timmerbreeks' (coward).
TIRRAVEE	Temper: 'She's in a richt tirravee: her puggie's up.'
TOON'S DIRT	Country phrase for city slickers.
TOON SPEAK	A locally notorious person, talk of the town: 'She'll no be pleased till she's the toon speak, that yin.'
TOOZIE	Unkempt; but 'a toozie tea' is a 'high tea' (with cooked meat).
TROKE	Business: 'Dinnae hae nae mair troke wi the like o him!'
TROWIE	A little troll (Shetland); also means 'sickly, third-rate'.
UG	To upset: 'Ah wiz fair uggit at him.' 'Hit wiz ugsome.'
UNCHANCIE	Unlucky, dangerous; also 'wanchancie'.
UNCTIONEER	Auctioneer.
UPTAK	Comprehension: 'He wiz nivver whit ye'd caw ''gleg i'th' uptak''.'

VEET	Veterinary surgeon: 'Oo'll (we shall) need tae geet the veet.'
VENTERLOKIST	'It's no the cuddie at's speakin, it's the coo's a venterlokist; but ye kin see her lips movin!'
VEXT	Sorry: 'Oh, Ah'm richt vext tae hear that.'
VORE	Spring (Northern Isles).
WAMEFY	Stomachful: 'Ah've haen ma wamefy o that crood.'
WEE	Small: but also means 'weigh' in Edinburgh.
WEE-BOOKIT	Small and skinny.
WEEL-BOOKIT	Big-bodied.
WEY O DAEIN	Method: a favourite Fife expression.
WHEECH	Whip (off, or away): 'Wheech aff yer dram!' 'Ah cannae: some'dy's wheecht it.'
WHIGMALEERIE	Crotchet: drinking game of 'turn-about' in asking posers. Revived as name of Radio Scotland quiz.
WINSHIN	Courting: 'Aboot the time 'at Ah wiz winshin the wife...'
X-RAY	Old Edinburgh newsboys' call when selling extra editions.
YAP	Apple, in Edinburgh 'keelie' slang.
YAWKER	'Rock' used as missile; also 'yuck'. 'A sowster o a yuck' is a large stone.
YIP	Impudent but insignificant person: 'Nane o yer cleck, ye yip!'
YIVTY	You are ordered to do something: 'Yivty go fur Paw's paper, Maw says.'

ATSAW RANOO!
(That's all for now.)